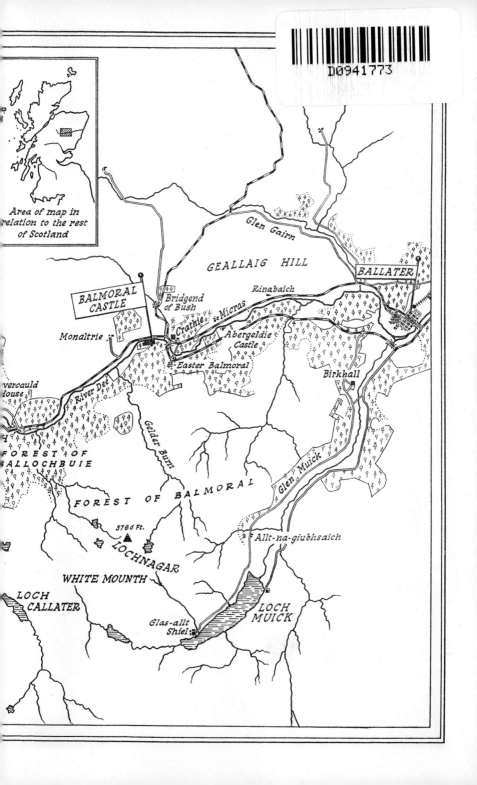

Area of map in
relation to the rest
of Scotland

GLEN GAIRN

GEALLAIG HILL

BALLATER

BALMORAL
CASTLE

Bridgend
of Bush

Rinabaich

Crathie · Micras

Monaltrie

Abergeldie
Castle

Easter Balmoral

Birkhall

vercauld
House

River Dee

Gelder Burn

FOREST OF
BALLOCHBUIE

Glen Muick

FOREST OF BALMORAL

3786 Ft.

Allt-na-giubhsaich

LOCHNAGAR

WHITE MOUNTH

LOCH
CALLATER

Glas-allt
Shiel

LOCH
MUICK

BALMORAL

Balmoral

The History of a Home

BY

IVOR BROWN

COLLINS

LONDON AND GLASGOW

FIRST PUBLISHED 1955
THIS IMPRESSION 1966

PRINTED IN GREAT BRITAIN
COLLINS CLEAR-TYPE PRESS : LONDON AND GLASGOW

Foreword

FOR HELP in the writing and illustrations of this book I am greatly indebted to Her Majesty the Queen for her gracious permission to have photographs taken inside Balmoral Castle and also to Sir Alan Lascelles, at one time Private Secretary to King George VI and the present Queen, and to his successor in that office, Sir Michael Adeane. For any errors of fact and taste I am myself wholly responsible.

All the photographs are supplied by Mr. James Reid of Ballater, except that of Queen Victoria and John Brown, which is from the Picture Post Library.

For my chapter on "theatricals" at Balmoral I have been greatly helped by that grand veteran of our stage, Mr. Allan Aynesworth, who was there as far back as 1896 while he was working with Sir George Alexander and the St. James's Theatre Company. For accounts of later visits I have been much aided by Miss Eleanor Elder of the Arts League of Service Travelling Theatre, by Mr. David Steuart of the Perth Theatre, by Mr. Alec Robertson of Dundee, and by the present manager of the Dundee Repertory Company.

My thanks go also to Eric Linklater for permission to quote from his book *A Year of Space* and to the house of John Murray for similar permission in the case of Queen Victoria's *Journals*.

The spelling of Highland place-names varies so greatly

that uniformity can only be achieved by altering the quotations in which they appear. Lord Byron's Loch-na-Garr is Lochnagar on most maps of to-day. Queen Victoria hyphened it as Loch-na-Gar. In the Ordnance one-inch-to-mile map of the Cairngorms those mountains are spelled both as two words (Cairn Gorms) and one. The same map spells the loftiest of these as Ben Macdhui, while Bartholomew prefers Ben Muich Dhui. That was the form used by Queen Victoria. She also wrote of Loch Muich which is now commonly spelt Muick and pronounced Loch Mick (an English victory?). There has also been continual uncertainty about the linking of the Craigs and Glens with the names following. To some Glen Gairn is Glengairn and so on. Furthermore, the Craigs are Creags in the form used by some writers and cartographers.

As I think alteration of quotations undesirable, I have left the spellings varied. So Lochnagar and Ben Macdhui will be found in various, slightly different forms. But since there is never any doubt as to the mountain or glen in mind, there is no confusion of meaning and that is what matters most.

1955   I. B.

Contents

Illustrations

9

CHAPTER ONE

Balmorality

"AT a quarter past seven o'clock we all arrived at dear Balmoral. Strange, very strange, it seemed to me to drive past, indeed *through*, the old house; the connecting part between it and the offices being broken through. The new house looks beautiful. . . . An old shoe was thrown after us into the house for good luck, when we entered the hall. The house is charming; the rooms delightful; the furniture, papers, everything perfection! "

Such was Queen Victoria's entry for September 7, 1855, in her *Journal of Our Life in the Highlands*. Her own Balmoral, hers and her Consort's, not that old Balmoral held on lease, was in being at last, three years a-building and now in occupation. In the following year she proclaimed her overwhelming joy in this creation and possession. " Every year my heart becomes more fixed in this dear Paradise and so much more so now that *all* has become my dearest Albert's own creation, own work, own building, own laying-out, as at Osborne: and his great taste and the impress of his dear hand, have been stamped everywhere."

" Everything perfection. . . . This dear Paradise." There was no gush of insincerity, no false exaggeration about that. The *Journal* is one of the happiest books ever written, despite the fact that in its second volume it covers a period of intense grief and mourning. It is a record of " unforgettable days," an appreciation not only of the scenic sublimities of Upper Deeside and the Cairngorms, but of family fun. " How I wish we could travel about in this way and see *all* the wild spots in the Highlands! We had gone thirty-five miles, having ridden nineteen and a half! The little girls were in great glee the whole time." This after a northward journey in which even the ghillies, Grant and Brown, did not know the way. " I was delighted to go on *à l'improviste*," wrote the Queen, eager for the unknown. She was on the top of glorious hours when she mounted her pony, with John Brown attending, with Prince Albert armed for the chase, and with the children in glee.

There was, inevitably, the pain of parting. The Queen's dread of the return to England was as poignant as any child's distress at the end of the holiday with the menaced return to a school disliked. " Alas, the last day! " she wrote on September 18, 1858. " I wished we might be snowed up and unable to move. How happy should I have been could it have been so! " There was snow about and brilliant sunshine followed it, making to-morrow's separation from such beauty even more of an affliction. " Oh, how I gazed and gazed on God's glorious works with a sad heart, from its being for the last time, and tried to carry the scene away well implanted and fixed in mind! "

Balmoral and the Great Expeditions made from its Castle evoke a continual rapture from one whose London life had been at first tightly constrained by a watchful mother and then burdened with the cares of a sovereign before such cares were natural and due. We most of us love the Highlands " when the clouds lift, and the infinite heaven breaks open," when the summits are all visible and the rocks are burnished by the sun. But Queen Victoria adored them in all weathers. Rain or shine—and there were numbing winds, shiversome drenchings and even calamities with upset carriages on the hill-track roads—from the shores of Loch Muick to the summits of Lochnagar and Ben MacDhui, it was all bliss. The Queen's vocabulary was not extensive, but it had intensity of joy. Perfection! Ecstasy! The words exultingly recur. But one had to be hardy to enjoy these raptures. Since Queen Victoria lived so long as an ageing and aged woman, we easily forget the extraordinary vitality of her youth. When Albert was nodding on the sofa after a hard day in London, the young Queen was ready to dance in the dawn and enjoy the spectacle of sunrise too.

Considering the happiness which Balmoral conferred both on their new owners and their tenants, it is odd, and most unjust, that the word Balmorality has been used as a weapon of attack by some Scottish writers in recent years and directed against follies and even crimes for which the new occupants of the Castle were in no way guilty. Because a single house was built beside the Dee, it is blamed and even cursed for some ugly episodes of Scottish history whose origin lay elsewhere and was of far earlier date.

The word Balmorality seems to have been invented by George Scott-Moncrieff who used it as the title of an essay in a volume, with many excellent contributions, called *Scotland in Quest of its Youth*. This was edited by David Cleghorn Thomson and published in 1932 during one of the periodic resurgences of Scottish Nationalism and with reference to the talk of a Renaissance of Scottish Art and Letters. The editor mentions the author of the " Balmorality " piece as being his youngest contributor, and youth, in this case, was certainly having its Highland fling. Mr. Scott-Moncrieff curiously assumed that the occupation of Balmoral by Queen Victoria was responsible for almost anything bad that happened in Scotland either then or later on. He even associated Balmoral with the infamous " clearances " of crofters to make way for sheep farms and later on for deer forests; these iniquities he described as " all quite in accordance with the Balmoral attitude." This is monstrously unfair. I can find no evidence that the Royal Family ever evicted anyone from their new demesne and much evidence that they were exemplary landlords and greatly improved the housing on their estates.

If I can interpret his whirling words aright he also found Balmoral responsible for any mistakes made in the architecture of Edinburgh. He ended up by comprehensively denouncing " the deadening slime of Balmorality, a glutinous compound of hypocrisy, false sentiment, industrialism, ugliness and clammy pseudo-Calvinism." So poor Queen Victoria, when she was attracted and delighted by the climate and scenery of Upper Deeside, was responsible for the Scottish response to the Reformation, to the Industrial Revolution, and the latter's defacing of the lands between Forth and Clyde with the squalour still sadly visible. As these events either took place or had begun to take place considerably before the royal descent upon the Dee, the relevance of this tirade is indiscoverable and the essence of it is not only offensive but absurd. These are but the foolish observations of an emerging pamphleteer; the author— now a gifted writer on Scottish landscape, architecture and other native topics—would hardly, I hope, republish them to-day. They are relevant only because the title he gave to his essay has stuck in the familiar manner of mud that has been flung and is continually reappearing in the disputations of Scottish intellectuals.

It is true that there was a succeeding cult of " bogus " Scottish life, true that a proliferation of Highland apparel began to appeal to a wide range of tastes, in and out of Scotland. But this donning of unnecessary kilts and bonnets and waggling of unnecessary sporrans in a pseudo-Caledonian masquerade, though it has greatly irritated trousered Scottish journalists in the Scottish towns, does not seem greatly to have distressed what was left of the Highlanders. In any case, Queen Victoria's first delight in her new home was not caused by Scottish grandeur but by Scottish distaste for pretentiousness. One of the earliest visitors at Balmoral was the diarist Greville who testified to Queen Victoria's delight in the simplicities and sincerities that she found in Scotland; amid her new happiness she was almost naïve in the ingenuous acceptance of all things Highland; here was a happy exchange from ceremonial and Court routine.

Balmorality is blamed for the elaboration of the old Gatherings into the highly publicised Games, now so packed by motor-coach and private parties and followed on circuit by semi-professional athletes and trained pipers and dancers from the barracks and the towns. But it was a simple Gathering that the Royal Family attended at the Castle of Braemar on September 12, 1850. " The Duffs, Farquharsons, the Leeds's and those staying with them, and Captain Forbes and forty of his men who had come over from Strath Don were there. Some of our people were also there." By modern standards it was a midget matter. The stone was " put," the hammer thrown, the caber tossed, and there was the ghillies' race up Craig Cheunnich, accomplished in six minutes and a half, and won by " our ghillie, Duncan."

Then came a move to the Castle and " a pretty reel by Mr. Farquharson's children and the Ghillie Callum, beautifully danced by John Athole Farquharson. Mamma, Charles and Ernest joined us at Braemar. Mamma enjoys it all very much: it is her first visit to Scotland. We left after the dancing." There was nothing pompous, nothing " bogus " about these early manifestations of the Balmoral way of life and the enjoyments to be found in the old, wild strath that was now to be Royal Deeside.

The race up the Craig was later on abandoned because it was, in the Queen's sympathetic opinion, too severe. Some of the runners spat blood after this gruelling climb and the victorious Duncan suffered a permanent weakness from the punishment he had given his lungs and heart. With this ordeal removed, the early Braemar Gatherings were, in fact, " fun and Games," almost a family party, as local and intimate as the village Games of Scotland still are in unfashionable places. If the abolition of privacy and distance by motor transport and the fierce pressure of modern publicity have altered all that, it was certainly not the fault of Queen Victoria; her ideas of a Highland holiday are not to blame. The object of her quest was simple isolation; even Balmoral was not lonely enough. She had to escape further, to a bothie on Loch Muick.

It is a constant irony of our times that the search for solitude so quickly involves the destruction of it; the modern public dearly loves a Beauty Spot and immediately makes it far from beautiful. In the same way the new settlers in Balmoral may have provoked a bogus Scottishness in those who insisted on pursuing them. But their own devotion to the lands of Mar was as authentic as the beauty of Olivia in *Twelfth Night*, " 'Tis in grain, sir. 'Twill endure wind and

16

weather." Those who surmount the Cairngorms or bivouac on the shores of Loch Muick will certainly have wind and weather to endure.

The despised " Balmorality " includes the favouring of tartans and, with some cause, the salesmanship of the hideous, tartan-covered " gifties " and gee-gaws which have, on occasion, been made in Switzerland, and are now an odious article of commerce in the major cities and the " tourist " villages of Scotland. But the Queen's affection for tartans, so lavishly indulged in clothing and in up-holstery, was at least a liking for something genuinely and uniquely Scottish and she is hardly to be censured because a later commerce covered toys and trinkets with tartan for the travellers to send home labelled " frae yont the Border." In any case the salesmanship of tartans had begun long before Balmoral was taken over and rebuilt. When George IV visited Edinburgh in August, 1822, not only was he clad as a Stuart, but an ex-Lord Mayor of London, Sir William Curtis, was also prancing about the city in a Stuart kilt, to which he had no claim at all. Thus Balmoral can hardly be blamed for kilts ordered and for capers cut a quarter of a century before it was taken over.

Few will dispute that a piper in a bedraggled kilt attempt-ing a pibroch outside a London " pub " is a miserable spectacle. Of the same, sad kind is the Grand Highland Panorama seen in a music-hall or during a pantomime with its display of such " weaves " as never were on moor or glen; pitifully foolish are the kind of Caledonian attire and antics popularised by Sir Harry Lauder, whose genius for communicable song was not accompanied by any reluctance to make his fellow Caledonians look like zanies on the stage. A Lowlander himself, he promoted the idea among the

English that the workmen of Clydesdale habitually went a-roaming in the gloaming clothed like the chieftain of Clan McCrazy. The proper name for this type of Highland fever is not Balmorality, but Tartanitis.

The early Gatherings at Braemar, as was explained, were of an indigenous, elemental kind. So was the pursuit of deer and grouse. The last thing that the Queen would have wanted during her beloved escapes was a September Deeside Season, with an influx of London Society, accompanied by photographers, gossip columnists, and news-reel cameras. Especially would she have deplored the massing of motor-transport and of gaping spectators round Crathie Church on a Sunday morning. She was, no doubt, the indirect cause of a Highland vogue which has developed its tiresome, tawdry, and vulgar aspects. But an indirect cause is no proper recipient of censure for accidental results. The Queen and the Prince Consort went to the Highlands for refuge and recreation—recreation in its true sense of being made anew. Of the depths and warmth of this felicity, achieved on high, cold places, in the forest of Ballochbuie or on the summit of some of Scotland's most lonely and most lovely mountains, there is no possible doubt. What reason or justice can there be in the grumbling of embittered Scots because Scotland was thus intensely and sincerely beloved?

It must be remembered that the young Queen and her German Consort were not yet assured of popularity in the South: they had continually to be on their guard against making the wrong move and giving offence. Here, at Balmoral, they were away from the cold and searching glance of criticism and the nagging necessity to be incessantly circumspect. No less important was the fact that here, in Balmoral, was something which they had found for themselves and had, moreover, made for themselves.

Ghillies and foresters there were in residence, good men to take over. But otherwise there was no established and tenacious staff of royal hangers-on; there were no ancient " dug-ins " holding to their considerable " perks " and privileges. This was a great boon, especially to Prince Albert who had devoted himself, at great expense of worry and fatigue, to clearing up domestic muddle and waste at Buckingham Palace and at Windsor. The control of the Royal Household had been divided between the Lord Steward and Lord Chamberlain, political noblemen who came and vanished with the sway of Parties and the change of Administrations. " In Buckingham Palace," Lytton Strachey records, " it was believed that the Lord Chamberlain had charge of the whole of the rooms with the exception of the kitchens, sculleries and pantries, which were claimed by the Lord Steward. At the same time the outside of the Palace was under the control of neither of these functionaries, but of the Office of Woods and Forests: thus, while the insides of the windows were cleaned by the department of the Lord Chamberlain—or possibly in certain cases of the Lord Steward—the Office of Woods and Forests cleaned their outsides."[1]

There was divided control—or rather divided anarchy— in all staff matters, which meant complete lack of order and discipline, gross overstaffing and appalling waste. This assured not luxury but intense discomfort to the Royal Family and their guests. Strachey further records, " The Queen observed that there was never a fire in the dining-room. She inquired why. The answer was ' The Lord

[1] Lytton Strachey, *Queen Victoria*, p. 132.

Steward lays the fire and the Lord Chamberlain lights it ';
the underlings of these two noblemen having failed to come
to an accommodation, there was no help for it—the Queen
must eat in the cold."

For the Prince, a foreigner and suspect, to invade and
tidy up this world of bitter jealousy and squalid intrigues
was a wearing task. He was bound to make himself hated in
the precincts and to set more tongues talking actively against
him below stairs as well as above. But he persevered. How
great then the relief to get away from all this inherited and
inherent pride and privilege of petty-minded and self-seeking
ushers and menials! At Balmoral it was possible to build
up a household and its staff from the start and the human
material was very different from that of the quarrelsome
Household officers and of the Servants' Hall barnacles in the
royal houses of the South.

Balmoral offered a complete escape from the odious world
of Yellowplush and of the lackeys-in-waiting who were more
concerned to be gentlemen than waiters. Willingness,
honesty and dignity were delightful substitutes for the
indiscipline and corruption that Albert had so diligently
fought. Here was family life and with it familiarity. In the
case of the manservant John Brown who " commenced as
ghillie " in 1849 and " entered our service permanently in
1851," and whose " care and faithfulness cannot be
exceeded " familiarity, said the never-to-be contented critics,
went too far. But the Queen valued him for possessing " all
the independence and elevated feelings peculiar to the
Highland race," and for being " singularly straightforward,
simple-minded, kind-hearted and disinterested," with " a
discretion rarely to be met with." She may have discovered
in him virtues which others could not discern. She may,

later on, have overrated him absurdly, when he was promoted, in her widowhood, to be a permanent, personal attendant. But at first one of his attractions was to be an embodiment of the Deeside population, an aboriginal of " this dear Paradise." In Scotland he was John Brown, of the Bush Farm at Crathie, not a Palace Malvolio. The latter he did, it seems, become. But the corruption of the best is often worst.

There is continual praise in the *Journals* for the High-landers with their lack of the obsequious touch. To enter a farmhouse, or a cottage, was to meet a frank welcome with more courtesy than curtsy. " Come awa ben and sit down, Queen Victoria," the women would say. Or, " Is this you, my Sovereign ? " Old Mrs. Grant, a ghillie's mother, said to the Queen, on her entrance to the Grants' house, " I am happy to see you looking so nice," and this way of expressing affection was found touching and gratifying. So far from being an imposition of regal London on the Highland scene, the retreat to Balmoral meant an achievement of intimacies and popular contacts impossible elsewhere. The modern nuisance of the standing, staring crowds was not then a harassing presence. Political Ministers might have to be present, but the *Journal* says little about them. It is much more concerned with the country-folk with whose work and feasts and sorrows there could be a close and easy participa-tion.

The way of the eminent among the ordinary is always difficult. If the former keep aloof, they may be charged with pride; if they mingle, they may be accused of patronage. There is often an opinion of the lowly that the high-ups should behave as such: yet, if the high-ups do stay loftily apart, this may be no less resented. How are gifts to be bestowed and kindliness practised without risking a sneer at Lady Bountiful? Balmorality is the kind of term that could be flung readily at the royal entry to the humbler Aberdeenshire homes and at relish of the ghillies' way of life; it would have been flung none the less had there been a chilly segregation behind the Castle gates. It is a tribute to the supreme tact of the Royal Family that the problem of blending sovereign status with the approach to all has now been so well solved. In the social climate of the eighteen-fifties, with the monarchy open to a sneering criticism never heard to-day, it was no easy matter to do the acceptable thing. Balmoral made the right touch at least less difficult.

The intermingling of the Castle and the cottar folk was carried on without embarrassment on either side. There was no condescension when the Queen drove up to the Bush Farm, whose tenants were the Brown family, in order to watch them " juice the sheep." Equally unceremonious was the attendance at a cottage christening of the forester's child. After the baptism, the Queen wrote, " I gave my present (a silver mug) to the father, kissed the little baby, and then we all drank to its health and that of its mother in whisky which was handed round with cakes. It was all so nicely done, so simply, and with such dignity."

Dignity is here the important word. It was this quality in their new acquaintance that both the Queen and the Prince especially esteemed. They themselves avoided processional pomp. To another christening the Queen drove with her two daughters; Prince Leopold sat " on the box " with John Brown. There was no second carriage for him. There was, in less happy circumstance, the Queen's anxious part in the search for the body of a child called Jemmie

Rattray who had been drowned by falling into the flooded waters of the Dee. After this tragedy the Queen " drove up to the Bush to warn Mrs. William Brown never to let her dear little Albert run about alone." These quiet friendships and relationships were not possible in the English palaces; they were natural to " our Highland Home." At Crathie, the village outside her gates, she could " belong " and to do so was to gain a new experience of the human race after the early sense of remoteness and imprisonment in grandeur.

It is significant that, when the mature Queen was becoming more awesome, it was to the highly placed in blood or politics, to the Prince of Wales after a misdemeanour or to a statesman after too loquacious an interview, that she showed her aptitude for curt severity. While she stiffened in her attitudes in one phase of her life, she relaxed in others. Increasingly she allowed herself to be advised, talked at, and even ordered about by the man from the Bush Farm of Crathie. The theorists who allege that the privileged John Brown had become, in some degree, a symbol of the dead Consort, because Albert had been, at least in the days of his best health, so entranced by his days on the hills with the guns and the ghillies, are surely being overfanciful. Brown had little enough in common with the studious slave of conscience and the tireless worker among docketed papers that was Prince Albert. But he did symbolise the Highlands and the sturdy independence which Queen Victoria so warmly welcomed at and around Balmoral, though she was by no means so fond of this quality when encountered elsewhere and especially in politicians. So Brown could later on be forgiven his brusqueness, his interference, and even his insolence, because his presence took Deeside to

Thames-side and carried the dear Paradise among the braes of Mar to the much less dear Castle above the playing-fields of Eton. It is surely a happy compliment for Scotland that the Queen insisted on taking a Scottish accent in her train, though she had, because of her duties, to leave the country itself, with anguish, in the autumn.

Her attitude to Balmoral was deeply sentimental while she stayed there and poignantly nostalgic when away. In indulging her affectionate emotions to such a degree she was, indeed, being true to the country whose landscape and aboriginals so stirred her feelings. For the Scots, though fairly reputed to be canny and calculating, manage to be richly sentimental at the same time. This is a fact which infuriates those Scots who are pained by the presence of a melting mood and regard any show of devotion to national tradition as a bogus rapture and a form of Balmorality. Unless the depth and warmth of Scottish sentiment and its frequent dominion over calm reason be admitted, how can we understand the creation of, and loyalty to, the legend of Stuart nobility and chivalry which some members of that House and even the Bonnie Prince, after his short and splendid hour had passed, did so much to falsify and make ridiculous? Queen Victoria took especial pride in the slender trickle of Stuart blood in her veins and rejoiced in being as much a Jacobite as a German-speaking Hanoverian. Her infection by Tartanitis was severe because the supposed kinship with the picturesque and the spirit-stirring clans, however fictional, brought warmth and comfort to one ready for the extremes of sentiment.

" Tho' something like moisture englobes in my eye " is a villainous line of verse written by a poet great in his own parish, but apt to fall heavily when he left it. Coming from a Scot, it describes accurately enough the tearful yet dulcet melancholy of a race whose favourite pipe-music is a lament, whose most hard-worked adjectives are bonnie and wee, and whose home-thoughts from abroad have composed some haunting lyrics of the heartbreak kind. It was Robert Burns, Scotland's darling, who wrote that phrase about opthalmic conglobation, in a line which, with all its absurdity, would have pleased Queen Victoria much more than certain others from the same liberal pen. Burns has become the perennial Laureate of Scotland because, with all his libertinism and his defiance of the Holy Willies, he could be gushingly ethical too.

> " *To make a happy fire-side clime*
> *To weans and wife,*
> *That's the true pathos and sublime*
> *Of human life.*"

The Queen could have been as safe and happy with Burns in this mood as she was with Lord Tennyson. To this dewy-eyed, domesticated Caledonia she could respond, indeed did respond in Crathie village, as though she were a genuine daughter of Deeside. The " weepy " side of Scottish sentiment is none the less real because it can so easily become tedious.

Certainly she was never a Ruth, sick for home, standing in tears among the alien heather. Prince Albert, conifer-conscious, found the scenery and the forestry of Western Aberdeenshire very much to his taste because it reminded him of Germany and Switzerland. He did much, by encouraging plantation, to increase the likeness and also, less happily, to stimulate the rainfall. But Victoria had no need to strengthen her Caledonian raptures with botanical and geographical comparisons. She could respond spontaneously to the Scottish moods and feelings, especially to the kindly gusts of maternal benevolence inherent in a language where " wee " is the ubiquitous epithet of affection. What to her husband was a landscape with happy arboreal associations was to her an emotional home. Did she read her Stevenson in later life? If so, when once more pent up in London, she might well have murmured to herself, with some moisture conglobing in the eye:

" Blows the wind to-day, and the sun and the rain are flying,
Blows the wind on the moors to-day and now,
Where about the graves of the martyrs the whaups are crying,
My heart remembers how."

For " the graves of the martyrs " read " the cairns of my dear ones," and these lines would perfectly bring up the vision of Balmoral with its family memorials on the hills.

The Scottish Muse has thriven on the homesickness of a nation much dispersed; it has been, in a way, happiest when least happy, ocean-divided and dreaming of the shieling on the misty island; one of the most tender visionaries about native bens and burns, Charles Murray, author of *Hamewith* (Homewards), wrote from Africa in the dialect of, and in devotion to, the Donside lands which lie just to the north of Balmoral. It is significant that Stevenson, with the moor winds blowing in his memory, did not speak of a recollecting mind. For him it was " My heart remembers how." And so for Murray it was a case of " Hamewith, back where the heart is a' the time." Pathetically simple is the Scot's yearning:

26

" *There's a wee, wee glen in the Hielan's*
Where I fain, fain would be;
There's an auld kirk there on the hillside,
I weary sair to see."

This burst of " wee, wee " sentiment is no example of
Scottish verse in its loftier utterance of the absentee's regrets.
Charles Murray usually wrote much better than that in his
yearnings from the veldt for the Howe of Alford in spring
and the later glow of heather upon Benachie. I quote the
inferior passage to show that the royal writer of the Highland *Journals*, whose leaves seem almost to be wet with
tears when Balmoral was to be left behind for another
winter, was in her spiritual home when she poured out her
devotion to Deeside with a flood of italics and exclamation
marks. If the detested Balmorality includes excessive flow
of soul about all things native, the true Balmoralists are the
authentic sons of the Auld Mither and not only the Royal
Invader.

Another, and a curious, fact about the sharp critics of
Balmorality, a tribe very difficult to please, is their suspicion
that a happy Scot must be a traitor to reality and that to
achieve felicity in fine surroundings is in some way dis-
creditable or even nefarious. While they cannot endure the
moist eye of the man of sentiment, they are even more
infuriated by the sound and spectacle of Caledonian laughter.
One of their habits is to hurl the word kailyard at any piece
of writing which offends against their severe dislike of a
sob or a smile in the picturing of their native life. Because
the new Balmoral made its first owners extremely happy and
also stirred their feelings to copious expression, I have heard
it called " that Kailyard Castle."

No argument about Scottish writing can continue for ten minutes without somebody alluding to the Kailyard, a term which must continuously mystify readers or listeners who live outside the borders of Scotland. So an explanation must be given. According to George Blake, who has made a special study of the matter in an admirable little book called *Barrie and the Kailyard School*, the lines

> " *There grows a bonnie brier bush in our kailyard,*
>   *And white are the blossoms on't in our kailyard* "

came from " an old song that was done up by Robert Burns and contributed by him to Johnson's Museum with the air picked from the singing of a country girl." Ian Maclaren, the pen-name of the Rev. John Watson, one time Free Kirk Minister of Logiealmond in South Perthshire, began in 1893, with the encouragement of that extremely sharp-eyed editor, William Robertson Nicoll of *The British Weekly*, to publish sketches of parochial life in a village which he called Drumtochty and which was close, in spirit, to Logiealmond. The banks of the Almond, as students of Trinity College, Glenalmond, and travellers from Crieff to the Central Highland by " The Sma' Glen " discover, are pleasant and incline, when the sun is warm, to pleasant thoughts. The Rev. Mr. Watson, though he disguised his name and profession, could hardly concentrate upon the darkness of human nature, the bestialities of sinful man, and the squalors of Scottish pastoral life. In any case, public taste was not then tolerant of the scabrous in fiction and, if he had concentrated on the fornications of his flock, of which he may have had some inkling, he would not have satisfied either the editorial judgment of Robertson Nicoll, the readers of popular British magazines, or the astonishingly widespread public overseas whom his Drumtochty sketches and subsequent works delighted.

He had chosen as the title of his first volume *Beside the Bonnie Brier Bush*, quoting the lines about the kailyard and the white blossoms. At the same time his success and Robertson Nicoll's acumen, both as editor and publisher, created a vogue for nice stories about the queer, picturesque Scots and their doings amid the very picturesque scenery which was faithfully reproduced on acres of canvas in the studios of successful Royal Academical painters. The stories need not necessarily be happy: Maclaren had a taste for death-bed scenes and could deal ably with the pathos of the brilliant young scholar, well tutored by the village dominie, who goes up to the University, triumphs in the exams, and dies of meritorious exhaustion. But the tales had to be decent, uplifting stuff, showing the quality of the Scots' talk—but not in so broad or so authentic a form as to be unintelligible to alien readers—and using the rugged humours of Scottish country life.

Maclaren's success was followed, on a rather higher level, by James Matthew Barrie of Kirriemuir. There was also S. R. Crockett, a Galloway man born at Little Duchrae, just north of Kirkcudbright, and later a Free Kirk Minister like the Rev. John Watson who became Ian Maclaren. Crockett wrote (with a less enduring success) in two styles. One was in historical romanticism, as in *The Raiders*; the other was a sugary handling of the Boy Meets Girl story, as in *The Lilac Sunbonnet*, whose heroine is called Winsome Charteris. The anti-Balmoralists were certainly given something to work upon when they maintained that Scotland was being sold to the outside world as a swarming ground of pawky elders, viewed only as character-parts, and of never-to-be-adult juveniles.

The phrase Kailyard, picked from the Brier Bush rhyme, appeared in W. E. Henley's *New Review* in 1895 as a contemptuous description of the village idylls of Maclaren's Drumtochty and of Barrie's Thrums and of the Romances of Crockett's yarns about roamers in the Galloway gloaming. There was a case for the punishing use of the Kailyard label, but, like many useful labels, it came to be tied far too often to innocent parties. It was applied, quite unfairly, to anybody who did not belong to the Midden and Misery School of Scottish writers who were determined that henceforward there should be no more Kailyards and only Muckyards. The short-lived George Douglas Brown had led the attack on Kailyard sentiment powerfully with *The House with the Green Shutters*; he was followed at intervals by others who gave the impression that Glasgow consisted only of the Gorbals and that the Drumtochties were considerable rivals in vice to the cities of the plain. Finally, the anti-Kailyard fury began to insist that there should be no happiness or tenderness or laughter left in the depiction of Scottish life.

In 1954 the Saltire Society of Scotland, which exists, worthily, to preserve and develop Scottish traditions and talent in the arts, to strengthen national feeling, and to sustain the best elements in the Scottish way of life, began to publish its own review. Almost sixty years after the creation of the Kailyard label this tired sneer was continued in an astonishing article by Mr. Walter Keir, then holding a teaching position in Aberdeen University. In his second paragraph he was already citing the phrase " Balmorality " and quoting a passage from the essay by George Scott-Moncrieff on that topic, an essay in which Scotland is described as " repopularised by Scott and adopted as a plaything by a foreign queen." Scott, apparently, should have kept quiet in order to satisfy the austere tastes of Mr. Scott-Moncrieff and his dislike for making Scotland liked, while Queen Victoria should never have fallen in love with Deeside. Since Mr. Keir, while he admits that this essay is biased, claims it to be true in its main outline, he apparently approves of this suggestion that Queen Victoria's deep affection for a noble piece of country, for its mountains, for its people, and for her adopted home among them, was nothing but an infantile addiction to a doll's house.

Surely nobody who reads the *Journals* with any sympathy for the pressure of feeling behind the simple words can doubt the reality of the love for a place. But Mr. Keir is not so weak or so old-fashioned as to read with sympathy. Later on in his article, after alluding to the Highland romances of William Black who came before Maclaren and Crockett, he says, " The Victorians loved this sort of thing and all the more after Queen Victoria's adoption of Balmoral and *her own ventures into the field of fiction in her Journal.*" The italics are mine. I quote it as typical of what anti-Kailyardism and the sneering at Balmorality brings about. The Queen is accused of being a liar when she set down, for private purposes, her record of " the never-to-be-forgotten days." Sir Arthur Helps, who persuaded the Queen to publish what she had written for her family and her friends, attested " the perfect faithfulness of narration," adding that in every page " the writer describes what she thinks and feels rather than what she might be expected to think and feel." Presumably, in the opinion of Mr. Keir, Sir Arthur was party to a contrived deception. Mr. Keir is entitled to his own views, but it shocked me that the first number of the *Saltire Review*, which could rightly claim to be an important publication and has an Advisory Board of distinguished Scottish writers, should have carried this accusation, unsupported by any instances of falsehood, that the *Journals* were merely fictional.

The same article contained both derision and patronage of Sir Compton Mackenzie, " precariously poised on the remains of a very genuine talent." It was Sir Compton's " romps " that stirred this academic distaste and one can see plainly that what really angers the type of Scot who cannot forget the Kailyard or stop nagging at Balmorality is the presence of gaiety in the Scottish scene or the Scottish picture of the scene. The writers of that race are scolded by this school of critics, as we saw, if they shed a sentimental tear; they are found equally culpable if they proceed to invent a fictional romp or to echo the sound of laughter in the clachan or the glen. Because William Black in *Wild Eelin* or Crockett in *The Lilac Sunbonnet* wrote sickly romances more than fifty years ago, there are not only to be no more romances, but no more comic inventions either. The function of the novel, says the same article that damned Queen Victoria's " fictions," is " the presentation of the real situation in society at a given time." Sir Compton should apparently be ashamed of his romping and settle down to the kind of sociological research that would get him a Diploma in a School of Economics. In other words, the novel is to be primarily a factual treatise in which narrative values are negligible. The old craft of creating characters and telling a story has ceased to count. Small wonder that John Buchan is written off along with Neil Munro.

That a Scot contented is a Scot contemptible is the essential view of the misery-mongers who lump Balmoral

QUEEN VICTORIA BY WINTERHALTER
Portrait hanging in Balmoral Castle

THE PRINCE CONSORT BY WINTERHALTER
Portrait hanging in Balmoral Castle

in with the wretched creations of the Kailyard. To those tortured by the spectacle of human happiness the confessions of bliss made unashamedly by the royal settlers in Balmoral were unendurable, and even incredible. So the *Journals* must be fictional. It is, of course, easy to smile in a superior way at the *naïveté* of some of the composition. The Queen protested to her editor that she had no skill in writing and that her records were just " homely accounts of excursions near home." So they are, but what emerges for the unbiased reader to-day is an impression of simple, abiding, unaffected joy in the exploration of the Highlands and in the exchange of the London Palace for the Scottish home.

Scotland has no reason to be ashamed of having conferred, through its people and its landscape, its food and its drink, serenity and recreation. (I use recreation in its proper sense of making one feel born afresh.) It has rendered this service to many people of all kinds and long may it do so. Recording a day on which Ben MacDhui was ascended, the Queen wrote of unforgettable pleasure, despite " lunch in a piercing cold wind." Later on she stated, " I had a little whisky and water as the people declared pure water would be too chilling. We then rode on without getting off again, Albert talking so gaily with Grant. Upon which Brown observed to me in simple Highland phrase, ' It's very pleasant to walk with a person who is always content.' "

Always content!

" *Canst drink the waters of the crispéd spring?*
  O sweet content! "

Dekker's hey-nonny song was written to console him that " patiently want's burden wears." It was not for kings and queens. But it suits the mood of the mountaineering and the Great Excursions from Victorian Balmoral. No doubt all the parties to the journey were not so happy. " I and Alice rode part of the way, walking wherever it was very steep. Albert and Bertie walked the whole time." The latter, Albert Edward, Prince of Wales, then eighteen, may not have been so gay as his father as he plodded up to the stony summits of the Cairngorms. But there were the ghillies, the whisky and " the crispéd spring." O sweet content, a felicity unforgivable by certain curious Scots and unbelievable by one of them.

CHAPTER TWO

The Chosen Spot

THE first journey of the Queen and the Prince to Scotland, which began at the end of August, 1842, had been a delightful experience, a voyage of discovery in which the crock of gold was indeed found at the end of the rainbow-vision. It was the discovery of the Highlands, first met in Perthshire, that created so much happiness and implanted the desire, a powerfully growing desire, for a home in these delightful recesses, far from the madding Court. The revelation had come chiefly at Taymouth Castle where the Marquis of Breadalbane entertained with all the pageantry of a chieftain's equipage. The scenery made the most agreeable and suitable background for the piping and the kilted parades. " The *coup d'œil* was indescribable." Such was the verdict of Queen Victoria as she looked through a casement at Taymouth and found the view magical.

In 1866 the widowed Victoria came back *incognita*, as she often cared to travel, to revisit in a quiet way the spot where her exploration of the Highlands had so blissfully begun. She wrote that " As we could not have driven through the grounds without permission and didn't wish to be known " she and her ladies looked down from a hill

" on the scene of our reception twenty-four years ago by dear Lord Breadalbane. . . . Albert and I were then only twenty-three, young and happy. How many are gone that were with us then! I was very thankful to have seen it again. It seemed unaltered." The Castle has since altered, at least in function, very much: it has been used as an experiment in hotel-keeping, it has been occupied by Polish troops, and it has been a base for the organisation of Civil Defence. The parks and lawns between the Castle and the Tay, whereon the massed pipers provided the young Queen with her *coup d'œil*, have become a golf-course, which, if not of championship standard, has exquisite turf and makes easy walking, with holes not too lengthy, for the senile striker of the ball.

Prince Albert's habit, already mentioned, of rejoicing in European parallels, found the Breadalbane lands of those years—" From Kenmore to Ben More the land is a' the Marquis's "—to be not only extensive but pleasantly reminiscent of Switzerland. In providing such European memories Taymouth had a partner in Penrhyn Castle in North Wales; another likeness was met with at Ardverikie, on Loch Laggan, where a drive along the Kingussie road " reminded us much of Thuringen."

The Ardverikie visit was made in 1847 and from it followed, owing largely to a climatic disaster, the leasing of Balmoral, farther to the east. The arrival in Scotland was made by sea; the Royal Yacht was used to carry the Royal Family, now growing, up the Irish Sea to the Clyde, round the Mull of Kintyre, and past Islay and Jura to Oban. A trip was made round the Isle of Mull to Staffa and Iona. There had been, so far, good sailing. " It was," wrote the Queen in her simple and endearing way of recording a happy experience, " the first time that the British standard with a Queen of Great Britain with her husband and children had ever entered Fingal's Cave." No serious trouble with the elements so far; then came a change for the worst. At Fort William they landed from the yacht, whose comforts, as well as the Hebridean panorama, received high commendation. There was a drive up Glencoe and later a stay at Lord Abercorn's house of Arkverikie. And then the weather did not so much break as collapse in cataracts.

The evening in Glencoe had been " excessively cold and showery " and this glen, under cloud, can be as sinister and saddening as it can be exhilarating on a day of clear sky. The arrival at Loch Laggan was made " in pouring rain." With her usual charity towards all things Highland, the Queen recorded that the view was beautiful, but " obscured by rain." Although the house itself proved to be " a comfortable shooting-lodge," full of antlers and Landseers, the visit was a failure and even the royal hand, so ready with its raptures over the Scottish scene, became almost immobilised at the writing-table. " There is very little to say of our stay at Ardverikie, the country is very fine, but the weather was most dreadful." The Queen was left alone—with the rain; the Prince had to go north to Inverness, where he praised the hospitality of the Baillies at Dochfour, the lofty grandeur of the waterfall at Foyer beside Loch Ness, and the skilful continuation of the Caledonian Canal. He made no report of having seen a monster disturb the surface of the loch; but visibility was doubtless very poor, for the weather again was execrable. The Atlantic depressions were rolling in without cease or mercy.

When the return voyage was begun from Fort William

it was " very squally," at Crinan " it rained the whole time,"
and Lochgilphead " was reached in pouring rain." At
Campbeltown the conditions were no kinder and various
plans were considered for the yacht's run to shelter in case of
still heavier storms. A passage was made to Loch Ryan
with " the yacht rolling considerably " and off the Mull of
Galloway the vessel started, for a change, to pitch, still amid
pouring rain. " I was very ill," wrote the Queen. " Albert,
however, stood it perfectly and the children very tolerably."
Of the Mull of Galloway she added, " This was our last
glimpse of dear Scotland."

Dear Scotland! What a profound affection must have
been there to yield so warm an adjective after so cold a
welcome. Anyone else might have consigned this shiversome and soaking Caledonia to all the fires of hell. The
Queen was not a grumbler at Scottish weather as a rule, but
on this occasion the continuous downpour flooded even the
contented pages of the *Journal*. It might still be " dear
Scotland," but the fate of Ardverikie, once considered as a
possible site for the Queen's Highland home, was settled.
This region had seriously blotted its repute. Of what avail
the unquestionable beauty of the scene if the obscuring rain
prevented it from being seen at all? The accident of an
appalling September in this area was also to deprive the
West Highlands in general of a royal settlement, despite
the glory of the sea lochs and the allurement of the isles.
Better news had arrived—from another place.

While the torrents were falling in the west, Upper
Deeside was having the golden autumn weather which, when
it does come to the Highlands, is perfection. The clouds
had been caught and held in the west. On the eastern side
of the Cairngorm barrier there was a long spell of brilliant

sunshine. It so happened that the son of Sir James Clark, the physician in attendance on the Queen, had gone to Balmoral to stay with its lessee at that time, Sir Robert Gordon. The young man had been ill and was seeking a cure. He informed his father of the radiant days by the Dee and of the great improvement in his health owing to the purity and dryness of the air. These reports reached the Queen and Prince Albert as they returned to England with such moist remembrance of their month farther west. All thoughts of Loch Laggan were abandoned. Next year it was to be " Eastward " for them. Sir Robert Gordon's sudden death in 1847 made the house of Balmoral available and the lease was taken over from the Earl of Mar. On Friday, 8th September, 1848, the Queen made the first Deeside entry in her journal. " We arrived at Balmoral at a quarter to three."

After a meal, the first walk was taken. The scene, " reminding us very much of the Thuringerwald " was found to be enchanting, " wild, but not desolate." Everything looked much more prosperous and cultivated than in the not-yet-forgiven region of Laggan. " The soil is delightfully dry." Stags were moving near the house, but not near enough for Prince Albert's unsuccessful rifle. The animals came down quite close to the house later on, as it were to mock the frustrated marksman. But it was agreed that the choice of spot had been rightly made. The air was fresh and bracing and " all seemed to breathe freedom and peace." There was such an excellent staff awaiting them, Macdonald who in his kilt " looked a picture, remarkably tall and handsome " and Grant, the head keeper, who had been twenty years with Sir Robert Gordon, and was to be much approved by his new employer for his " fine, intelligent countenance " and " singular shrewdness and discretion." There was the young John Brown about the stables and making his way up, but he was not mentioned yet in the *Journal*. With the rain holding off and the Deeside ghillies showing up so well, it was a fine start for the new home, the paradise-to-be.

" Wild and yet not desolate." It was a shrewd summary of the landscape to which an accident of climate and a happy decision had taken them. It is the particular quality of Deeside to combine great heights around the river's source with a gently broadening valley in its middle life. The Dee falls rapidly from its springs in the Cairngorms, where there are wildness and desolation indeed, to become the famous salmon river descending amid forests to the fertile lands of the lower Strath. In a few miles it has passed from the waste to the arable; in little more than sixty it has moved from the Wells of Dee on the summit of Braeriach, at a height of over 4,000 feet, to join the sea at Aberdeen. Thus the area through which it so speedily travels is both essentially Highland and essentially of the sea coast and the plain.

To call Aberdeen a Lowland city would be to create a false impression among those who regard the lowlands as southlands. But its culture had been for centuries a thing of its own and its speech has been a particular brand of Scots which owes little to the Gaelic and much to the Nordic strains in Scottish life. Aberdeenshire, accordingly, is a county in which the two Scotlands of east and west make a handsome meeting instead of the old ferocious clash. It was here, at Harlaw near Inverurie, that the great drive of the Western Gaels, led by Donald of the Isles in an effort to overrun and enjoy the fertile shire, was defeated, with the aid of cavalry, by the lairds and burgesses of Aberdeenshire in 1411. This victory for the East enabled the shire to prosper in agriculture and the civic arts while the Gaels kept their own speech and their own way of life in the mountains farther west.

So there was a rightness, due perhaps more to chance than to choice, in the selection of Aberdeenshire for the sovereign's Scottish home. A county of this widely inclusive kind held everything of Scotland's quality, ranging from the second highest of its mountains and the finest of its deer-forests to the rich, stock-breeding cattle farms of the centre, and the famous fishing ports of the shires east and north. In the district of Buchan Scotland can be seen as a windy plain where good farming fights hard weather: around Braemar there is the vast wilderness of Scotland's snowy rooftop. Thus, without making any exhausting or time-wasting journeys, the new tenants of Balmoral were able to achieve the solitude for which they especially craved and yet to be in touch with a considerable city and seat of ancient learning.

One day might be spent on the summits of the Cairngorms and the next in the company of the Eminent Minds gathered at Aberdeen. In the September of 1859 Prince Albert presided over the meeting of the British Association while the Queen was on her favourite peak. Here is her report:

" I heard by telegram last night that Albert's reception was admirable, and that all was going off as well as possible. Thank God. I ascended Loch-na-Gar with Alice, Helena, Bertie, Lady Churchill, Colonel Bruce, and our usual attendants, and returned after six o'clock. At ten minutes past seven arrived my beloved Albert. All had gone off most

admirably; he had seen many learned people; all were
delighted with his speech; the reception most gratifying."
(The Duke of Edinburgh has followed a fine tradition by
also addressing with distinction the same gathering of
V.I.P.s—scientific). The Association was entertained at
Balmoral a week later. The Queen described huge carriages
and omnibuses laden with " philosophers " arriving at the
Castle. She walked and talked with the leading *savants*,
and entertained them with Highland Games, somewhat
spoiled by a cold wind. Some of the learned stayed to dine
and sleep but " four weighty omnibuses filled with the
scientific men " drove off. The Queen seems to have been
as much impressed by the bulk of the visitation as by the
height of the arriving brows.

Braemar, at the top of the Strath, lies immediately under
the greatest of the mountains; Balmoral, nine miles to the
east, is less enclosed by the Cairngorm mass and the heights
that mark the Perthshire boundary. It has spaciousness and
the superb prospect of Lochnagar which does not overlay
the Castle but provides, at a pleasant distance, the finest
possible backcloth for a summer twilight. The river-lands
start to broaden out at Ballater, ten miles farther east, and
then begins the typical Deeside landscape, expansive and
rhythmical in the great sweep of heathery and partly
forested hills.

It is the width and openness of Deeside that makes it so
attractive to many. There is room for cultivation to make
a contrast with the severity of the surrounding hills. There
is never the sense of suffocation which one may suffer in the
narrow Highland glens when the rain-clouds are drifting
like heavy smoke at a height of only a few hundred feet
and the sky seems to have become a dark, dripping, and

immovable blanket. Bad weather in Deeside can be bad enough, but it is not so crushing or dispiriting as it may be in the deep canyons of the west where the hills rise sheer on either side of a glen which is no more than a narrow slit among the cloud-capped rocks. Furthermore, because the Strath is not enclosed by peaks insurmountable except on foot, there is good access to the North and, after Aboyne, to the South. Queen Victoria, with her passion for travel and her enjoyment of scenery, was thus able to find more and better roads for her great expeditions than she would have done in the wilds of the north-west. She was discovering that desired peace without suffering an excessive isolation. She had, as it were, the poetry of Scotland amid the lofty sources of the Dee and among the Gaelic-speaking crofters and ghillies of that region, while the rich and reasonable prose of the cool Aberdeen mind was by no means far away, even in the days of the horse carriage.

There was, of course, no railway up Deeside in the years of taking over. In 1848 the building of the line had not reached Aberdeen and, when the Queen wished to return to London by train in late September of that year, instead of going home by sea, she had to travel as far as Montrose by carriage: there was no Royal Train then and a slow progress was made with stops for sleeping at Perth and Crewe. Rapid progress, however, was soon made with railway construction and by 1853 there was not only a line to Aberdeen but a beginning of the Deeside line which ran as far as Banchory, some sixteen miles to the west. So the weighty loads of scientific men did not have to burden their horses all the way to Aberdeen in 1859. The Queen obviously did not encourage further progress and the line reaching up to Ballater was not in use until 1867. It has never gone beyond that, and perhaps an extension to Braemar would have been uneconomic: in any case, it would hardly have been popular at Balmoral. " Not desolate "—but a certain amount of desolation was desirable. " The British Ass." might drive up on occasion, but too much of that kind of thing was outside the holiday programme.

The region of Balmoral, incidentally, was not without its own claim to scientific distinction. In 1805 there was born at Inverey, a village on the stripling Dee before it reaches Braemar, one John Lamont. He was sent away to school at the Benedictine monastery of Ratisbon, showed brilliance in mathematics, won an academic post at Munich, and became a celebrated astronomer. It seems that his loyalty to the land of his fathers was not strong: this flower of the forest did not long for a return to the Cairngorms; his heart was not in the Highlands. He changed his name to Johann van Lamont and is buried near Munich. But he had given Inverey the familiar caption of the countryside paper— " Local lad makes good."

Had this member of Clan Lamont returned to the base of the Cairngorms in his later life he would have been coming back to what was still a rough and primitive society. The " friction of exalted minds " might be momentous down the river at Aberdeen, but upstream the way of life was hard and poor. Mrs. Lindsay, the daughter of Dr. Robertson, the first Royal Agent for the Balmoral Estate, has left, from her memories of childhood and youth, a striking picture of the regional poverty and the absence of comforts and amenities. At the end of the eighteenth century there was but one carriage in the three parishes of Tullich, Glenmuick, and Glengairn. The crofts, or holdings, were of ten or twelve acres, the agriculture was primitive, and the staple diet was milk and oatmeal. Clothes were mainly homespun and the houses were two-roomed hovels of rough stone and earth, with damp, earthen floors and heather-thatched roofs. The windows could not be opened, but ventilation was amply provided by cracks and draughts. " During the first three or four decades of last century the common wage of a female domestic servant was from three to four pounds a year, and for a man as groom, gardener, or farm labourer, £10 to £12, exclusive of food."[1] One can hardly blame the many fugitives who, like John Lamont, preferred to find and keep a more abundant life in other countries.

Visitors to Scotland, if passing through Kingussie on the main road through the central Highlands to Inverness, should stop to see the Highland Museum which has been arranged by Miss Grant. There are reproductions of the old Highland " housing," if that is not too flattering a word for the dark crannies in which the Highlanders and Islanders have managed to live: in addition to these frightening places there are also fascinating examples of their handiwork, their furnishings, and the various household and agricultural implements which the inhabitants contrived to make and use. To mitigate the hardships of the life described by Mrs. Lindsay, the life, that is, which Queen Victoria and Prince Albert were going to encounter and to improve, there were the remnants of the clan system and its semi-paternal relations. Often there were remaining bonds of kinship and identity of name linking the laird and the tenant and their relations were by no means purely financial. The laird was still a chieftain and carried a chieftain's responsibilities for relieving distress and helping the sick. The Cash Nexus of the Industrial Revolution had not come to Crathie.

---

[1] *Recollections of a Royal Parish* by Patricia Lindsay, p. 8.

There was some growing of flax and spinning of it by the housewives who had profited, rather slowly and reluctantly, by the efforts of Lady Sinclair to train them in the right methods. She had even set up a little school of textile instruction in Braemar. As a less exemplary exercise, there was a long tradition of illicit distilling in the glens and, though the Excise Officers had got the better of their opponents by 1840, it is recorded that there were still a few practitioners at work and that the masons who were em-employed in the erection of the new Balmoral were refreshed at popular prices through the efforts of one Charlie Stewart, nicknamed " The Princie." It is believed that in 1821 two million gallons of whisky were distilled in Scotland unknown to the Government and without licence: it is unlikely that so remote a district as Upper Deeside, with its high reputation for turning the water of its burns into something better, should have been reduced to a wholly meek and law-abiding condition in another quarter of a century. Moreover, the district was well equipped with Drove Roads along which ponies carrying " ankers " of spirit, i.e. kegs containing twenty pints, could make their way at night to the centres of sale. Where the motor coaches now grind up the Cairn-well to the Devil's Elbow and the Spital of Glenshee, there used to be moonlight flittings with a convoy of such anker-bearing animals escorted by Highlanders carrying useful cudgels and the like.

The Drove Roads, which were the arteries of Highland life, still carried the great herds of cattle when they were moved down from the North to the " trysts " at Crieff and Falkirk. The herdsmen travelled about twelve miles a day and camped as they could: many landowners welcomed the beasts for the manure they left behind them. The drovers from Speyside would work by Tomintoul to Crathie and then either turn right for Braemar and the Spital route to Glenshee and Blairgowrie, or left for Ballater and Aboyne and the roads for the South. In either case the people living round Balmoral would be well accustomed to these autumnal migrants and would be watching their own property with care. Cattle-thieving was such a well-established sport of the Highlanders that to increase their herd as they went would be a natural practice; the herdsmen were poor men and likely to acquire good appetites as they tramped: so it was well to look to the poultry. Crathie itself had two annual fairs for the sale of cattle and sheep, while Braemar had three.

Although the insurrection of 1715 had begun at Braemar and some of the local lairds had been involved in the '45, there was little, if any, Jacobite sentiment waiting to be provoked by the arrival at Balmoral of a Hanoverian sovereign. One of the facts of Scottish history most difficult to explain is the readiness of the Highlanders to enlist in the British Army so soon after the disaster of Culloden and the ensuing persecutions. But join they did. Flora Macdonald did not appear to be surprised or indignant that her husband should fight for King George in America and, well before that war began, the Highlanders had been in arms for the same dynasty. During the Seven Years' War Lord Chatham, realising that Highlanders bred beyond the capacity of their land to feed them, suggested to the King the recruitment of these men to the King's service. The recent troubles and resentments did not hinder a ready enlistment.

From Deeside more than two hundred men rapidly joined The Black Watch in which Charles Farquharson of Inver-

cauld held a commission. When the Gordon Highlanders
were formed in the latter half of the eighteenth century,
there was a flow of recruits from the Highland hinterland
of Aberdeen as well as from the city itself. Despite the long
continuance of a British military garrison at Mar Castle,
there seems to have been little anti-English animosity. The
prickly type of nationalism is more apt to influence intellectuals than active and hungry young men with a living
to earn, barren acres—and few of those—to cultivate, and
too many brothers and sisters already in the home. So the
relics of the clans took the English King's shilling and
apparently did not regret the transaction. When Queen
Victoria came among them she was most welcome; that she
was ready to be more Scottish than the Scots did not,
apparently, annoy Deeside. Only those who must keep
carping at " Balmorality " seem incapable of forgiving her
for her addiction to tartans and bagpipes as well as to the
mountains and the moors.

There was a considerable number of Roman Catholics in
the district, but they were plainly not disloyal to the new
régime. In the middle of the nineteenth century there were
378 Catholic worshippers in and around Braemar, while the
Parish Kirk of Crathie had a membership of nearly 800.
The population has dwindled since then, as has so dismally
occurred all over the Highlands, and that despite the extra
employment on the Balmoral lands provided by the royal
occupation. I was told in the village shop of Crathie in 1954
that, in the memory of one still living there, very many
chimneys had ceased to smoke. But those remaining have
a much higher standard of living than had the folk of the
glens described by Mrs. Lindsay, with their dark little
houses illumined only by the light of a " cruisie," an

48

VIEW OF BALMORAL CASTLE

TWO VICTORIAN INTERIORS AT BALMORAL   *The ballroom*

The drawing room

iron lamp holding train-oil with a floating pith of rush for a wick.

The Protestants maintained an intensely austere discipline and late Georgian Crathie was no home for hilarity or for those with any appetite for other pleasures than the rewards of sober and industrious living. The Sabbatarianism was especially severe. Public rebukes were administered by the Elders to farmers who even moved a foot on the Sabbath. To have stayed all night searching for a lost beast on the hillside and then walked home on Sunday morning was regarded as a most heinous offence. Only a few years before the Queen's arrival the practice of dancing was vigorously censured, especially if the subject were mentioned on the Lord's Day. On 30th July, 1825, at the Kirk Session, as the Rev. John Stirton cited in his history of *Crathie and Braemar*, published in 1925:

" Alexander Lamond, Lochnalar, was rebuked and admonished for having in December last, on the Lord's Day, immediately after public worship, openly proclaimed at the church gate, a *ball* to be held at his house in the course of that week. The Session, considering this *profane practice as a most shameful outrage upon Christian feeling* and all decency, resolved, in order to put a stop to it in the parish, to treat all who should in any way promote or countenance balls in such a manner, as persons under church censure."

Seven years later, on 16th December, 1832, there was an even more fiery denunciation of the flagrant hedonism that sent people on country walks and even to meetings for revelry:

B.
D

". . . the Session met after sermon, and being constituted by prayer, took into serious consideration the *deplorable laxity of morals*, which seems to be fast gaining ground in the parish, particularly among the young people. And in reviewing the various causes that may be regarded as contributing to this growing evil, they cannot but consider in this light the profane practice of *idle strolling through the country on the Lord's Day*: *and also frequenting meetings of merriment and revel under the appelation of balls*, which meetings are generally convened near about the time they ought to be dispersing, and consequently are frequently kept up during the whole night—a practice that requires only to be duly considered in order to be peremptorily condemned by every sober and well-thinking person, especially on viewing the disgraceful system of profligacy and bastardy which it fosters and propagates, on the ruins of virtue and the Christian character."

This imposing piece of Puritan prose continued with great vehemence and no little verbosity, ending with a threat of debarring from all Christian privileges any person who should " contumaciously persist in any of the profane and irregular practices here mentioned." Damnation plainly awaited those who would take a Deeside " dander," as the Scots say, in the gloaming of a Sabbath day. They were little better than the hoppers and skippers of the dance floor for whose salvation there was but the smallest hope. One cannot avoid a suspicion that some of the most godly of the Crathie folk can hardly have felt secure in the neighbourhood of a Queen who had always avowed her love of dancing and did indeed encourage Highland frisks on many an occasion, out of doors by torchlight and in the Castle or other country houses on nights of festivity. Did news reach these sour ones of that Torchlight Ball at Corriemulzie in September, 1852? The hosts were Mr. and Lady Agnes Duff, and there were " most animated reels." Sixty were present and the ladies were in evening-dress and the gentlemen all kilted. " A long way, certainly, in miles, I believe," wrote the Queen of this outing, but she found it all " admirably done " and was glad to have made the drive.

" Most animated reels," with the Highlanders screaming " Neesh, Neesh, Neesh," which meant " hip, hip, hip! " Some of the Crathie elders, unless they were so snobbish as to pardon in royalty what was scolded in the villagers, must have ground their teeth at the news of such goings-on and at the royal approval of them. But there is no sign that any Kirk Session composed for the better ordering of royal morals one of those classical indictments of sin of which the piety of Crathie was so productive.

One of the curiosities of human behaviour is the readiness of those who live in severe climates and in hard surroundings to deny themselves the reliefs which even the gentlest indulgence of the senses might afford. Surely it is understandable that those who live beside blue waters and under golden suns should say, " We have received such bounty from Nature that we must be the more willing to pay for it with at least a moderate self-discipline and personal austerity." But that is not the way of the climatically-privileged world. In Capua the Romans followed Capuan vices and the azure skies of Hollywood do not, apparently, conduce to any greyness of conduct or mortification of the sun-tanned flesh. In the same way, it would be reasonable for the men of the mountains, the chill winds and the grudging soils to seek compensation for their afflictions in some indulgence of the senses. But it is exactly in these districts that Puritanism proves most attractive and self-denial is most rigorously practised—at least in public.

I remember reading the reminiscences of one who had been a lead-miner in the English Pennines; that is (or was) one of the bleakest of all industrial lives, the work itself being most dangerous in its possible damage of the lungs, while the place of work—in the high, storm-swept moors and gills of North Yorkshire and Durham and Westmorland—is most uncongenial except to the more active holiday-makers in fine summer weather. The miners of whom he wrote lived in small, isolated communities and often had to stay at their cutting in the hillside during the week. Yet their rules of life were of the most austere kind and the chapel discipline imposed in the villages was such as to kill geniality and make even the day of rest a day of affliction. All impulse of youth was suspect, all pleasuring a surrender to Satan.

So, too, in Scotland, it is in the grimmest Highlands that this self-denial is most sternly counselled and very often quite successfully imposed. Where there is least chance of congenial society, the social glass and the meeting for a dance are the most feared and even forbidden. The mountain background of Balmoral imposes a hard life on all who till or keep flocks and herds there; the beauty seen by the summer visitor is long obscured by rain and cloud: the isolation, before mechanical transport came, was intense. Yet the good folk of Crathie's Kirk would seek no remedy of the bottle and the dance and, if the less good did so, the official scoldings were of a ferocity that outranged even the major maledictions of the Old Testament prophets. Of course in these circumstances the sinner goes from bad to worse: if he is going to be told of hell-fire to follow, he comes to the conclusion that he may as well earn it properly. The austere ethics of the wilderness, with the hatred of even a mildly merry meeting or even a moderate caper, are unintelligible. But they abide, with some exceptions. The gold-rush miner in the back of beyond, in scorching Africa or frozen Alaska, was never given to self-martyrdom. In matters of morality Dawson City was not a Highland village with the Kirk Elders as dictators of decorum.

By now the motor car has crashed its way through the Scottish Sabbath and the Crathie pietists of a century ago would be mightily, even morally, distressed by the invasive crowds careering up the two Deeside roads for a glimpse of church-going royalty and a good Highland lunch at Braemar. But it was during the reign of the righteous (in their own esteem) that the Queen came to Balmoral. Over the hills to the North, in Central Aberdeenshire, there was a good sprouting of Free Kirks after the Disruption of 1843 and from their pulpits came a strong cry for plain living and high thinking. (Plain living was all that the new Free Kirk ministers could afford; high thinking they could provide, since many of those who had ' come out ' were owners of ability as well as of a conscience.) It was into an atmosphere of ethics strict and narrow that the Queen was coming. It was just as well that some of her uncles were not on the visiting list. She had brought the right husband, a serious man who played Bach on the harmonium. Music of any kind might have seemed giddy to Crathie's denouncers of the dance, but, if music there must be, surely the harmonium would pass. Moreover, she liked a good sermon and her sermons came from the invited preachers, Scotland's best,

and not from the old folk " girning " away about the devilry
inherent in a dance.

Behind the chosen site was the great mass of the Cairngorms, soon to be mastered by their new visitor, mastered
on pony and foot and mastered for the raptures their wilderness would convey. These mountains have no splendour of
sky-stabbing peaks; their grandeur is rather of the precipitous corrie falling sheer to a loch below the vast bare
tablelands of the summit ridges. They yield their own
jewellery, chiefly the stones known by the Cairngorm name
which are yellow or wine-coloured crystals. Massive crystals
have been discovered and Queen Victoria bought one of
fifty pounds weight for a sum of fifty pounds. The precipice
on the north side of Loch A'an has been especially renowned
for its crystal deposits. To the young Victoria the spectacle
of eagles and ptarmigans, the red deer and the roe, came
fresh and exciting. She found cairngorms on Ben-na-
Bhourd (3924 feet), the nearest to Braemar of the monster-
hills. It was a clear September day with views to the sea as
well as westward into the Forest of Atholl. There was much
stiff climbing on foot, but all was " delightful."

It was a constant relief, this colossus of forest, stone and
snow, this noble vacancy. As yet no ramblers intervened,
taking a free night's lodging as now they do beneath the
shelter stone under Ben Macdhui and beside Loch Avon
and not afraid to make it their midwinter igloo, which may
be a dangerous undertaking. Queen Victoria became so
absorbed in the glory of the great heights that she missed
something which to me is equally attractive, the undulating
rhythms of copse and corn and heather in the centre of the
county. Her Great Expeditions proceeded from the chosen
site to chosen distances, southwards into Angus, westward

to Glen Feshie and Blair Atholl. Had she crossed over more into Donside and beyond, she would have seen a landscape more easily habitable and none the less beautiful in its own gentler way. Few Scottish territories of arable and pasture can have lovelier interruption by heather uplands than are provided by the Hill of Fare above Echt and by Benachie in the Garioch, farther north. Did she ever make the journey, no long one, to see the Garioch fields in their harvest gold and Benachie in its pride of purple?

The selection of Aberdeenshire was a happy one, as I have said, because it contains every Scottish element and the colour-scheme of the land between the Don and the Moray Firth has every contribution that Nature and cultivation can jointly make. There is an old rhyme which explains that

> *A mile o' Don's worth twa o' Dee,*
> *Except for salmon, stone, and tree.*

Stag might have been added to the resources of the latter river. The verse has point. The Don runs through fatter lands: it is the water-carrier to the famous Aberdeenshire farming. It is renowned for its trout. It has tributaries too, that give the trout fisher some of his happiest hours. Donside, admittedly, cannot compete with Upper Deeside in majesty, and majesty was what took Her Majesty's fancy. She loved the thews and bones and big assemblance of a country-side and the vast skeleton of the naked Cairngorm summits. To many Scots there is relief in a mixed view such as Galloway in the far south-west and Aberdeenshire in the far north-east afford, with hills and the sea, the mountain, the meadow, and the moor. But Queen Victoria, once she had met her first glimpse of Paradise in Perthshire, was

dedicated to " salmon, stone and tree." The Dee gave her
the first in abundance; the forest of Ballochbuie and all her
own adjacent woodlands gave her the third. As for the
second, stone towered above her in the form of Lochnagar
and allured her in half a dozen of Scotland's pine-girdled,
snow-capped giants. Also it lay at her feet, white and
sparkling, the granite of the Abergeldie quarries, the granite
to build the chosen home in the chosen spot.

CHAPTER THREE

The Home

THE name Balmoral was an old one. Stirton found the earliest mention of it in 1451, when it was spelt Bouchmorale. Thirty-three years later Alexander Gordon of Midmar paid the Crown annually £8 6s. 8d. for the tenure of Balmorain. The present spelling appears in a valuation of lands dated 1635. Either as Balmorall or Balmoral that has been the form generally used since them. The derivation remains disputed.

The origin must be Celtic. But was it Baile Moraile—the magnificent Baile or Bal? Baile or Bal is a common word for a place or township and is the prefix to many Highland and Irish names. Or was it Bal-mor-aol? In that case it would be the Place-Great-of-Lime. There is limestone adjacent. Or was it Bal-mor-choille, the place of the great woodland? The proximity of the great forest of Ballochbuie is an argument for this third surmise.

Which we choose is of little importance, since all explanations are relevant for reasons either of the view, of the geological surroundings, or of the adjacent forest. The name Balmoral has, for me at least, a comfortable sound. The pun with moral and morality has been exploited, as we have seen, by the critics of the so-called Balmorality, with the implication that the word morality suggests only the less desirable and more pretentious types of good behaviour. But, if we leave this now tiresome pun out of account, we have a fine, rolling sound. The mixture of the letters " o " and " r " has often made for dignity and beauty in our speech. It confers an atmosphere of glory and warm auroral sunrise, although I admit that Boreas can be cited against me: in October the union of letters, with the help of the effective " w " reminds me of Housman's lines:

> " *From all the woods that autumn*
> *Bereaves in all the world.*"

In all, it may be called simply a good, consoling name with a touch of comfort rather than of frigid ethics in its composition.

The present Balmoral Castle is at least the third of its kind, since the building which Queen Victoria first leased and then bought for demolition was not the first on the spot. The lands and big houses of Upper Deeside were for long shared by the Gordons and Farquharsons, with the latter dominating in the end. The former were not, or were not considered to be, true Highlanders; they were of Aberdeenshire and less of the Braes of Mar. Mrs. Lindsay puts it this way in her *Recollections of a Highland Parish*: " The Gordons were not of Highland origin, and it is curious to note that in the early part of last century the use of the Gaelic language had almost died out of their property; while on the north bank of the Dee, of which the Farquharsons—a Celtic family—were proprietors, the old tongue still held sway."

The Farquharsons had come out of the west, being originally men of Rothiemurchus. Romance continually attaches to them, as befits the man from the mountains. Heroism surrounds the name. The grandson of the first Farquharson to settle on Deeside fell at the battle of Pinkie while he was carrying the Royal Standard against the English. The clan was ever active in war and a Charles Farquharson was prominent—and wounded—in the wild charge at Killiecrankie. He went afterwards to Paris and the service of the Old Pretender—or King James III, as he would have claimed. His son, James, " Balmoral the Brave " was in the field in both the campaigns of 1715 and 1745; in the latter he was wounded fighting at the Battle of Falkirk and displayed characteristic gallantry by refusing to be carried from the conflict; this would be a waste of four bearers. So he ordered his body to be borne in the van of the fray. This seems, if one considers it, to be a little hard on his carriers, who presumably had to go forward and do combat under handicap of a stretcher. Perhaps we need not take the story too seriously; the romantic details may be discounted. But it is indisputable, in any case, that the Farquharsons were nearly always in " the thick of it." The " always " must be qualified, because one of the clan, Farquharson of Invercauld, did not " come out " in 1745; this eased matters after the defeat of the Jacobites at Culloden. But romance intervenes again with James's brother, Francis, who was taken prisoner at Culloden, removed to London, condemned to death and reprieved at the last minute owing—romance says—to the influence of a noble lady who had been much taken by his looks. It may be so. He was, in fact, spared.

The Cairnaquheen, Stones of Remembrance, can still be seen beside the Dee; they are, as it were, the last footprints of Jacobitism in defeat. The practice was for each member of the Clan that went out to war to add his stone to a pile. When the warriors returned, each survivor removed a stone; consequently the size of the remainder told the size of the casualty list. Balmoral saw a few more of the sad survivors of Culloden. Being on the old Drove Road, it was on the track used by some other fugitives. The men of Angus, under Lord Ogilvie, passed Balmoral on their way across the hills to Glen Clova. The Ogilvies had been in action in both the Jacobite campaigns.

Two more Farquharsons were to live at Old Balmoral and to live, it seems, beyond their means; great caution was needed, since one-time Jacobites had fines to pay as well as the ordinary costs of living. Caution, especially financial caution, is no cousin of romance, nor is it a mark of the Highlander in general. In 1798 Balmoral was sold to the Earl of Fife as the mortgage burden had become too severe, and the Farquharsons retired to the north of the river, their traditional stronghold. The Earl used Balmoral as a property for renting and so, in 1830, the Gordons were back as tenants in the property where they had been established during the fifteenth and most of the sixteenth century, until the Farquharsons took over.

The lessee this time was Sir Robert Gordon, brother of the Earl of Aberdeen who later became Britain's Prime Minister. Sir Robert had been a diplomat and British Ambassador at Vienna. It is unlikely that he ever committed any indiscretion owing to loquacity, since he was famous for his refusal to be a chatterbox. The Marquess of Aberdeen had left on record a remarkable post-prandial silence when three of the Gordon brothers had been dining together. At last the eldest remarked, " Robert, how loud your watch ticks." Yet the new Laird was popular locally;

great kindness accompanied his taciturnity and he had a voluble and hospitable sister in Lady Alicia Gordon, who was often with him and kept much company at Balmoral.

It was Sir Robert who created Balmoral II, assuming that what he took over in his Mar lease was the only house ever built on that site. Dr. Stirton says that " Sir Robert Gordon demolished the interesting old edifice which had been the home of the Farquharsons for generations and built practically a new castle in its place. The first additions were commenced in 1834. The kitchen, offices, and square tower or turret were added in 1838 and the whole building completed in 1839. The deer forest was made in 1833." Stirton further regrets the destruction of the " fine old manor " (Balmoral I) in order to put up a bit of architectural " gingerbread." Dr. Douglas Simpson in his little, but valuable, book on *Balmoral Castle and Crathie Kirk*, says nothing of demolition and mentions only " large additions." However that may be, this was the house which Queen Victoria and Prince Albert entered in September of 1848 as the new lessees; they did not become owners until 1852. It was, as the old pictures show, a jumble of styles, mainly baronial, but with a low-pitched, more domestic-looking wing. But a jumble is not necessarily ugly; sometimes the contradictions reach a visual agreement.

The Queen drove up by carriage from Aberdeen through villages where the party passed under triumphal arches and were welcomed with flags and cheers. She sat with the Prince and her two elder children in an open carriage. (The children were to become Empress of Germany and King of Great Britain. But at least they had their simple childish holidays by the Dee, before glory descended with its usual imprisoning grandeur.) Mrs. Lindsay who saw that arrival as a child remembered the Queen's " bright face framed in a simple straw bonnet, with a keen glance which seemed to take note of everything." Lady Augusta Stanley, however, said " they drove up smothered in blue veils." Professional reporters rarely agree. Why should amateurs? " Royal Stuart Tartan was conspicuous in the draperies of the carriage." Already that tartan upholstery! The haters of " Balmorality," if any had been present, would have had cause there for grinding of the teeth.

Balmoral II modestly provided a small hall, billiard-room, and dining-room on the ground floor. Up a good broad flight of stairs there was the old drawing-room: this was made into " our sitting-room, a fine large room," with the bedroom, opening to the Prince's dressing-room. " Opposite, down a few steps, are the children's and Miss Hildyard's three rooms. The ladies below and the gentlemen upstairs." The number of the ladies and gentlemen was not stated. The house, in pictures, looks larger than this description suggests, but it was not large enough if any entertaining were to be done, as of course it had to be. Steps, accordingly, had to be taken, for there could be no question now of moving to another and more accommodating house elsewhere. Balmoral had evoked love at first sight and a love that endured.

It was theirs on lease only for the first four years: in 1852 the house and estate were sold by the Fife Trustees for £31,500. There were 17,400 acres of land and the property stretched westward to the summit of Lochnagar. Demolition of the inadequate premises began in the following year and the foundation stone of Balmoral III was laid on 28th September, 1853, with a formal ceremony attended by all the workmen and domestic staff. There was a cavity in which a bottle was to be laid down containing a parchment record signed by all the family: it also held " current coins of the present reign." A trowel was handed to the architect, Mr. Smith of Aberdeen; the mortar was spread, the stone was lowered, and the bottle was sealed and interred.

Mr. Anderson, then Minister of Crathie, prayed for a blessing and toasts were drunk. It was a very windy day, but there were no mishaps. After the rites came the revels. There was a large staff dinner, followed by Highland games and a dance at night. " The dancing," wrote the Queen, " was performed with the greatest spirit." Some of those Elders, across the river in Crathie, must have had their loyalty strained. Dancing—and the Minister asking a blessing on company so ready for these corrupting capers! Prince Albert managed to take the afternoon off and escaped to Craig Gowan with his gun. His " bag " is not related.

Dr. Douglas Simpson properly disputes the notion that the Prince was the architect, a notion which has had some excuse in the Queen's delighted acknowledgment of " my dearest Albert's own creation, own work, own building, own laying-out, as at Osborne." That the internal arrangements and decoration should be determined by the Queen and the Prince was natural: they had strong views as to their new home, which was to be the " place " of a Laird and not the palace of a monarch. But amateurs cannot wholly replace architects in the arrangement of a considerable mansion, and it is not to be supposed that William Smith, son of John Smith who had been responsible for Balmoral II, was elbowed aside. He had a great position in his profession, both in the city and county of Aberdeen. Dr. Simpson comments on his particular skill in the handling of his native stone, granite. " He never tormented it with effects for which the material is unsuited, but boldly massed his rock-like masonry so that his buildings have something of the hard crystalline character proper to the stone. Above all, he was rigorous in his insistence on good craftsmanship. Everything about his buildings—masonry, woodwork, plaster, cast-iron, and lead—is of the highest quality and the most enduring character." The chief mason of Balmoral III, James Beaton, was a noted craftsman and, in the ashlar work, he had a master who would expect the highest standard.

Once when I was exploring the coast of Buchan to find an elusive Victorian house which had some ancestral connections, I gave the name of the place to a worker on the road on which I expected the building to be. I asked him what it looked like and he answered, " It's in the style of the period, massive." The word massive, spoken slowly, in a bass voice, and with a broad " a," is a very powerful epithet and massive a house on the eastern shores of Aberdeenshire must be if it is to be a proper shelter when the wind is tearing in from the North Sea. Balmoral, though it is over 700 feet above sea-level, is sheltered by the Deeside mountains and its own wealth of woodland and of lofty timber. But it is massive in case of climatic need: architect and mason saw to that. It is also " in the style of the period " since it can be labelled Scottish-baronial.

That is a fashion which has been much derided and was certainly much abused when the New Rich of Scotland's Industrial Revolution began to implant their " pepper-pot and ginger-bread " castles on the estates they had bought in the Highlands. There was no good reason why a shipping-magnate or a coal-owner who had bought a deer-forest should insist on living in a species of fortress vaguely suggesting that there were bowmen in waiting behind the splits of windows in the turrets. Having once lived for a year in the front quadrangle of Balliol College, Oxford, I learned that baronial slits are by no means good illuminants of a room modernly employed. In the case of Balmoral III there was an excuse for the use of this style. It was a castle replacing two other castles on a historic site; it was built when Scotland was still close to Sir Walter Scott and when the Romantic Revival in Scottish art and letters was still alive and was not just a stale tradition.

Nowadays we find the baronial towers ugly as well as antiquarian, but had Smith insisted upon, and had his royal clients accepted, a Scottish country mansion in the style of the brothers Adam, he would have been equally antiquarian. That each epoch should discover an architectural style of its own is highly desirable if such a variety of styles can be accompanied by a variety of excellence. But since so much of excellence, as well as so much of difference, is unlikely to be always available, we have to put up with much that is derivative and hope that the derivation will work out well. A Neo-Palladian Balmoral would have pleased many critics rather more than does the Neo-Baronial one, but it must be remembered that the classical style, while admirable in Edinburgh or amid the parks of a Border landscape, is not in tune with the scenery or the tradition of the Highlands.

Balmoral, in its setting and with its views to the tremendous and even terrifying crags of Lochnagar, could justly be built in that romantic style.

> " *England! Thy beauties are tame and domestic*
> *To one who has roved o'er the mountains afar:*
> *Oh for the crags that are wild and majestic,*
> *The steep, frowning glories of dark Loch na Garr!* "

B
E

Byron's point, made in a poem of his youth and not of his best, has value still. The lands that stretch up to the cluster of Scotland's central heights can reasonably demand an architecture related to a soaring wilderness, and not to a nook in a gently rural landscape.

The material was there, the granite in the neighbouring quarries of Glen Gelder, a granite remarkably white in colour. Amid the darkness of its surrounding woods, Balmoral stands up in luminous contrast. It is often said of the best domestic architecture that it appears to have grown naturally from the scene and to be seated on the landscape with the ease shown by a naturally good rider on his horse. Castles are, as a rule, things imposed on a site and not things evoked from it. They are there by command and to command. Balmoral III is certainly a building made to order for a royal purpose, but it belongs in stone to its country-side and in romanticism to the antiquity and severity of man's hard life among the Braes of Mar. The result may be dubbed " Balmorality " by those determined to find fault with all things Victorian, but it is doubtful whether the average wayfarer who looks across the river to the house or enters the gardens and sees it at close hand before the arrival of the Royal Family in August, is displeased with the spectacle. The clean, stern, windswept, rain-washed look of this White House among the pines and firs seems right enough if the mood and methods of the Romantic Revival are ever to be pardoned or permissible at all.

Though Balmoral III had to be more spacious than its predecessor, there was no idea of creating something vast; this was not to be a Blenheim of the North. The tower, it is true, is substantial, a hundred feet high by thirty-five feet broad. The largest room was to be the ballroom, 68 feet by 25 feet. The dining-room and drawing-rooms are smaller than those of many a seigneurial country house. The library is also of modest size. The original arrangement of the major rooms has remained; the advancing ideas of domestic amenity have brought minor alterations. The decorations, though naturally readjusted with changing owners, remain, on the whole, faithful to the founder's idea of a Highland home with all things Highland about it.

The critics of "Balmorality" could fairly claim that Highland dress and decoration were overworked by the new owners. Having arrived in a tartan-decked barouche on her first entrance to this Paradise, the Queen continued to spread herself in the invention of new "weaves" and in the use of her inventions as well as of traditional designs. The upholstery, the curtains, the chintzes, the covers of sofas and chairs, were either in tartan or had a thistle pattern. To carry lamps there were beautifully designed figures of Highlanders. Lady Augusta Stanley summed up the *décor* by calling it "all highly characteristic, but not all equally *flatteuse* to the eye."

The Prince designed the Balmoral tartan of black, red and lavender on a grey background. This is kept in use. The Duke of Edinburgh wore handsomely a kilt of this colour-scheme at the Braemar Games in 1952. The Queen arranged her own Victoria tartan, mainly employed in furnishings, and saw that the new Balmoral was be-tartaned from the linoleum to the roofs of the rooms. The Royal Stuart (red and green) was also favoured: there were carpets both of this and of the Hunting Stuart. The Queen saw nothing strange in this choice of clan, since, despite the presence of the Duke of Cumberland in her family tree, she

professed herself an ardent Jacobite and would never speak
of Charles Edward Stuart as the Young Pretender.

Before we censure the royal infatuation with old tartans
and invention of new ones, it is worth remembering that
from the beginnings of the nineteenth century the native
" weaves " had been lavishly exploited and added to by the
new Scottish textile industry; there never had been a strict
organisation and limitation of the varieties of clan wear
because in a region so poor as were many parts of the Highlands people will take what they can get. During the
Industrial Revolution prosperity came to parts of Scotland
and the techniques of spinning and weaving were mechanised.
This made a large output easy and potentially profitable.
New patterns were invented to meet the growing domestic
market and the sudden demands of the export trade. (After
the fall of Napoleon there was a craze for tartans in Paris
and naturally no questions would be asked there as to what
was correct or legitimate wear.) Soon it was conveniently
discovered that all sorts of people with far from Gaelic names
qualified for a kilt or a plaid because they belonged to a
" sept " or division of a clan. So the invitation to buy is
widely issued. Is your name Clark or Clarkston? Then,
say the obliging authorities, you are entitled to a Cameron
kilt. Is it Brown? Then either the Lamont or the Macmillan is at your disposal. It is really quite difficult to be
called by a name which does not somehow qualify for Highland status, at least in the eyes of the Trade. In any case,
there is no copyright in tartans any more than in Old School
Ties. You cannot be arrested for wearing the colours usually
associated with a College or a Club to which you do not
belong. Nor is it an offence against law to go habited as a
Highlander though your name and blood be nothing of the

kind. This indulgence makes things easy for purchasers with romantic inclinations.

Queen Victoria was not the first to be infected with the fever of Tartanitis. Her uncle, George IV, had imposingly appeared in tartan trews during his visit to Edinburgh when he was greeted by Sir Walter Scott. He had a sense of humour to help him carry off the scene. It is also true that many a tartan, whether a genuine Highland antique or an invention of the Lowland clothiers, does look extremely well, especially as a lady's scarf, or as a man's kilt, if the lady has the looks and the man has the build and carriage for these things. Not many would agree that a fashion of the early nineteen-fifties, which put so many young women into tight, stove-pipe tartan trousers, was always justified by the results. Too often they lacked the requisite appearance as well as the justification by race and names.

After the textiles, the pictures. Sir Edwin Landseer was a welcome visitor at Balmoral and his pictures were naturally welcome on the walls. Some of his best work, revealing his admirable draughtsmanship, is there. In these years he cannot be forgiven for " The Monarch of the Glen." Because he interpreted the romantic side of Highland life with a realistic technique, he has come in for more than his share of the sneers and jeers directed at the eminent Victorians. When romance and realism both fell into disgrace with the " advanced " critics there could be little chance for the man who had committed the further crime— as " advanced " critics see it—of pleasing the general public and finding a profitable market. Winterhalter's portraits were also favourites on the walls of Balmoral III—and justly so. They have authentic grace as well as suavity of style.

Despite some labour troubles the work on the Castle

moved apace, much faster, surely, than it would have done
a hundred years later when the grip of the Trade Unions on
the building trade was so strong. The new house—Castle in
style but home in the owners' affections—was hailed as
" dear Balmoral " and was deemed to look beautiful though
only half-finished. Parts of Robert Gordon's Balmoral II
were still in use for gentlemen-in-waiting and for the
accommodation of domestic staff. The first Cabinet Minister
to reside, Lord Granville, was promoted to a room in
Balmoral III. There were various advantages about the
new building and not of spaciousness only. It had far better
views than its predecessor owing to more skilful siting. Also,
its luck was in. How fortunate that only three days after the
entry came news of battle and of victory! Sebastopol had
fallen. The earlier muddles and humiliations of the Crimean
War were being avenged.

The stationmaster at Banchory had received the news by
telegraph and, since mechanical communications still ceased
there, he had to take the road. He mounted a horse and
galloped apace like Browning's riders who brought the good
news from Ghent to Aix; he had to cover thirty-five miles
with the telegrams for the Queen and Lord Granville,
presumably with a change of steed. He reached them at
half-past ten at night. Rejoicings were at once proclaimed.
Prince Albert was immediately dispatched to light a bonfire
whose raw materials were waiting on Craig Gowan. " All
the gentlemen, in every species of attire, sallied forth,
followed by all the servants." The fire on the hill blazed
conspicuously and there was a considerable din of jubilation.
The Highlanders were encouraged to go natively gay.
There was piping: there was whisky: Grant and Macdonald blew up a deal of ammunition by discharging guns

continually. Having a bang was a form of celebration not limited to the ghillies. A popular servant who had been taken over, along with a favourite dog called Monkey, from Sir Robert Gordon's establishment, did his best to contribute to the jovial tumult. This was an Alsatian, François d'Albertançon, who kept struggling to light squibs only to find them damp and their ignition impossible.

Albert declared the scene " wild and exciting "; but his sons had evidently filled their lungs with air and exercise so effectively during a long and happy Balmoral day that neither pipes nor guns awoke them at night. When finally roused, they insisted on a trip to the conflagration; so off the children went, among the skirling of the pipers and the bangs of the musketeers. It was a great family party for a great national occasion. Prayers to " bless this house " had been, it was felt, most happily answered.

Love, too, entered in. Prince Frederick William of Prussia had arrived on September 14th; presumably he already had something on his mind. The romantic surroundings were, in any case, such as to stimulate romance. A week later he spoke to the Queen about a marriage with her eldest daughter, the Princess Victoria, who was still only of school age, but highly intelligent and able to talk on level terms with her father about scholastic matters. The young man was ready to wait, but the Queen allowed, or possibly encouraged, immediate speech. Nine days later the Prince found a sprig of white heather during an excursion up Glen Girnoch; he put his question and found that his gift of heather was appropriate; the young man was in favour. The engagement was not announced formally until May of the following year. The Princess was married in 1858 while still under eighteen. So to Germany she went, but she remained, all her life, in German estimation and to the fury of Bismarck, " die Engländerin." As " the Daughter of England " she was detested by the Prussian reactionaries and Daughter of Britain, since Scotland should be included, she did, with half her loyalties, remain. Without doubt she was also misfortune's child.

Owing to previous planning and also to the words spoken by the banks of the Girnoch Burn, which runs down to meet the Dee between Abergeldie and Ballater, there was born, four years later, Kaiser Wilhelm II. This result may be set against the luck of Balmoral and its satellite houses on Deeside. It may be pleasant to speculate on the possible benefits to European history if Prince Frederick William of Prussia had found Deeside as wet as his mother-in-law found Loch Laggan, taken against the place and its schoolroom Princess, and fled in no mood for courtship. But such a dynastic union had influential backing and possibly, with or without this bride from Balmoral, the second Kaiser had to be. Without him Prussia would have found another of his kind.

Prince Frederick himself was an estimable man and a victim of destiny. He was lucky in his love, for the union was a marriage of true minds. But he was unlucky in all else. If the aged Kaiser William I had not lived so long, the Prince might have succeeded to the throne before Bismarck had become so powerful and so fanatical. Had that occurred, Frederick would have had some chance to realise his liberal ideas. He had the same outlook as his father-in-law and shared Prince Albert's vision of a free and progressive Germany. But he came to rule when already a dying man; his cancer of the throat, over which the doctors fought each other quite as keenly as they fought the malady, had been a long-drawn agony to himself and to his wife; his voice had gone and he could now only acquire power with the immediate compulsion to relinquish it. His son was on the Bismarck side, unruly and defiant in the family, a plague to his parents. We cannot put the blame for the First World War on a drive and " a dander " in the glen behind Birkhall and on the chance pulling of a bunch of white heather. But there the long journey to disaster and to Doorn may be said to have begun. The Princess lived on, as the Empress Frederick, to die of the same disease and to close in pain a life made wretched by the suspicion and hostility of the German Conservatives. But the star-crossed lovers of the Girnoch Burn had been lovers indeed and that private happiness was not destroyed by the cruelty of fate or the malice of their foes.

The royal selection of Balmoral in 1848 was to make this remote nook among the Central Highlands the scene of many hospitalities and also of political decisions made by guests of world importance. It was to bring nearly all the great figures of Whitehall to the village of Crathie and the Tsar of all the Russias to a sojourn among the Braes of Mar. It was to acquaint Mr. Gladstone happily with the Cairngorm summits, and less happily with the Queen's opinions on persons and on policy. It was also to set Mr. Disraeli, less active on foot and more adroit with his tongue, paying court to his Faery Queen under the curious eye of John Brown, the ghillie turned Queen's confidant and almost omnipotent factotum.

The first season at the new Balmoral ended with edification. The Rev. J. Caird had explained in the Crathie pulpit that real religion does not consist of moping over " good books "; it must be the active faith of the week-day and the girt-up loins, and not a contemplative creed of Sunday or of devotions in the study of a recluse. His sermon won the Queen's warm approval. She was usually delighted with the Scottish sermons and the simple service of the Scottish Kirk. All was going well with the soul as well as with mind, body and estate. By the time of next summer's return, Balmoral II had completely disappeared and only a memorial stone marking the old site remained. The new Castle was being embellished with bass-reliefs, the work of the tasteful Mr. Thomas, whose talent was much approved by Prince Albert. The subjects selected for sculpture were St. Hubert, St. Andrew, and St. George, symbolising the function of Deeside where the English join the Scots in the pleasures of the chase.

The story of St. Hubert has its curious aspect. Lost in the forest while still an ordinary hunter, he was rescued and shown his way by a benevolent and highly Christian stag who commanded him to give up his life thereafter to the service of the Faith. Hubert then became the Bishop of Liège and the saintly patron of the hunt. What he might have done, by way of recompense for his rescue, was to be censorious in the matter of hunting; what he did do was just the reverse; he gave hunting an odour of sanctity. But there he is in stone, to raise the ardour of the sportsmen of both nations when they set out upon a grouse-drive or a stalk. Once more one's mind turns to the Crathie Elders. Could it be right to have a Roman Catholic—a Belgian— on the walls of this neighbouring Castle? The Queen, it is true, had close links with Belgium through her uncle, King Leopold I. But were the canonised of Rome to gain a niche on the walls of the Protestant succession? National saints might be all very well; but St. Hubert was hardly of that magnitude.

So ended the first year of Balmoral. It had been made auspicious by the news of victory abroad and by the vision of love at first sight at home. How tiresome for the Queen to go back to Windsor and there to have to entertain the King of Sardinia who conversed—so queerly—about the health and strength of his illegitimate children and had, although uncouth, to be honoured with the Garter! What a descent from the altitudes, moral as well as geographical, of Deeside! At Balmoral the Highlanders did not talk like that, at least in company, and were altogether more fit for good society. In August of next year the Tower was finished and the gardens were getting into shape with the pretty Eagle Fountain so thoughtfully sent over by the King of Prussia. When October came and with it the dreadful necessity for leaving, "Albert was very busy, settling and arranging many things for next year." It was then that Queen Victoria wrote her often-quoted words about the fixation of her heart in "this dear Paradise."

The Scots, being well supplied with stony ground, are accustomed to expressing their emotions in monoliths, cairns, and the like. The erection of the Standing Stones, alone or in circles, was much practised by the ancient mariners and explorers of the Neolithic and Bronze Ages, as any wanderer in Scotland (and in Aberdeenshire not least) discovers. This habit persisted with the constant heaping of a humble cairn or the erection of a giant column surmounted by a statue. Since Germanic taste also favoured this custom, it was natural that the grounds of the new Balmoral should be freely covered with memorials in stone or stones, as well as in metal.

Not all these lapidary tributes were of a mourning kind. For example, no sooner had the property been bought than the happy occasion had to be celebrated with a cairn on one of the hills behind the house. This was Craig Gowan and thither on the morning of 11th October, 1852, went the family with all the servants and tenants, wives, children, and relations. Everybody had to pick up and place a stone and the cairn had reached a height of seven or eight feet when Prince Albert climbed to the summit and put the final touch. There was cheering, there was piping, there was dancing of " merry reels," even by the oldest: the gaiety was not conducted without imbibing. " There was whisky for all." The Queen ended her rapturous account of this " *gemutlich* " occasion by praying that God would bless this place and allow the owners to see and enjoy it for many a long year.

For herself the supplication was half-answered, but it was not answered at all for the Prince who died in the December of 1861. See it, she could; enjoy it she could not. Thus, for many years, the annual visits made bitter-sweet holidays. Hence ten years later there was another and most melancholy excursion to another knoll, Craig Lowrigan, to attend the foundation of another monument; this was to " Albert the Great and Good, raised by his broken-hearted widow." On it was " a fine, sharp pyramid admirably constructed out of granite without any mortar." The Queen and her " six poor orphans " laid their tributary stones and there it stands, a minor pyramid; though not beautiful, it is a sight to stir compassion as long as it may endure, since it is the symbol of a suffering that had no limit and no remedy.

It says little for a certain kind of Scottish Christianity that even this sombre piece of stone could provoke contentious bickering among the over-righteous. On it had been graven:

" He being made perfect in a short time fulfilled a long time;
For his soul pleased the Lord,
Therefore hastened He to take him
Away from among the wicked."

WISDOM OF SOLOMON, IV. 13.14.

The Rev. Dr. Candlish, of Free St. George's, Edinburgh, harshly criticised as irreverent this choice of a text from the Apocrypha instead of from the Bible itself. When certain newspapers, and correspondents in newspapers, supported the impertinent Doctor, the Queen might well have lost some of her profound affection for the Scots and Scotland. What would the attitude of these intense Bibliolaters have been if the Queen had preferred, or had added, some lines of secular poetry, say from " In Memoriam " ?

Inside the Castle there remains the marble statue of the Prince by William Theed. Albert was shown with a vigorous realism, in Highland Dress, prepared for the moors and ready to step out with gun and dog. A bronze cast of this was presented to the tenants and servants of Balmoral as a courteous reply to the memorial obelisk which they had raised. The bronze statue is near one of the entrances available to the public when the Royal Family are away; there is also a bronze statue of Queen Victoria. There are Celtic crosses in the grounds to commemorate the death of Princess Alice in 1878 and of the Queen's second son, Alfred Ernest, Duke of Edinburgh (as well as of Saxe-Coburg and Gotha), who died in 1900. There are cairns in memory of marriages in the family, and in the woods a statue of John Brown. Nor were the dogs forgotten in this profusion of statuary. "Noble, for more than fifteen years the favourite collie and dear and faithful companion of Queen Victoria" had his figure executed in bronze and set over his grave to the west of the Castle. Subsequent history has seen further monuments laid down, as the lives moved down the years and deaths, at home or abroad, removed the men of the Balmoral estates from the enjoyment of their Highland homes. Those who fell in the wars have their own Stones of Remembrance. There have also been plantings of trees to perpetuate the memory of visits or to celebrate an event. Few castles can have more majesty of varied timber than has Balmoral.

The gardens of the Castle have developed in beauty and in range of product down the centuries. They suffer inevitably from their height above sea-level, the lateness of the spring and the early coming of the autumn frost. This is not orchard country, but Scotland, much of the Highlands included, has long been famous for its soft fruits. Moreover, high ground, while it lacks warmth, freezes out pests that are common lower down. Hence it is possible to grow exceptionally fine and large strawberries at Balmoral and the unpunctuality of the crop is very well suited to the late arrival of the Royal Family after the London season has used up so much of the summer. There is also a late raspberry which is specially cultivated as a September crop.

Queen Mary, an assiduous connoisseur and delighted collector of all things rare and lovely, whether mineral or horticultural, left her mark of grace upon the Balmoral gardens. She loved to sit in a Summer House which has now become the playroom of her great-grandchildren; beside it is the enclave with a surround of rockery, rich in Alpines. This is known as the Queen Mary Garden.

The public has entry to the grounds on one day a week when royalty is not in residence. From the middle of June to the end of July is a good time for a drive up Deeside, since first Ascot races and then the climax of the London season, with the Royal Garden Parties at Buckingham Palace, followed by Goodwood and Cowes, make it almost certain that the grounds of Balmoral will be open to visitors. Walking amid the towering conifers one can hardly help visualising the grave seniors from Westminster who have walked there with their problems and the children who have scampered freely there while the gravity of problems was to them unknown.

> *" Ah! There my young footsteps in infancy wander'd:*
> *My cap was my bonnet, my cloak was my plaid,*
> *On chieftains long perish'd my memory ponder'd,*
> *As daily I strode through the pine-cover'd glade."*

The romantic Byron is less popular than the satirical and the sardonic Byron now. But, with the plashing sound of Dee below and with the open view across the lawns and over the menacing darkness of " the pine-cover'd glade " to " the rocks where the snowflake reposes," it needs a very unresponsive alien to reject altogether the raptures of which Byron sang and which Queen Victoria recorded with such charming innocence of style in her jottings about a world enjoyed.

CHAPTER FOUR

The Other Houses

THE Balmoral Estates now extend to 24,000 acres
directly owned; this includes Birkhall, at the Deeside
end of Glen Muick, but not Abergeldie Castle and its lands
which have been held on lease. There are also grouse moors
on the Farquharson land north of the river Dee which are
rented to Balmoral. Although Abergeldie Castle was not
in royal ownership, a great deal of money was spent on
improvements to the house, the estate, and the houses for
the workers on the estate.

Abergeldie is situated on the south bank of the Dee about
two miles east of Crathie; it has been a Gordon, not a
Farquharson, stronghold and has a very long and stormy
history. As early as 1378 Abergeldie was described as one
of the Aberdeenshire castles " of most respect." The old
mansions of Deeside were not merely fortified houses; they
had their service of the arts. Another in the " respected "
category was Crathes, near Banchory, the ancient home of
the Burnet family. The major part of that notable example
of genuine baronial is now open to the public on certain
days in the week and should certainly be visited as much
for its superb gardens as for the castle chambers with their
painted roofs and many fine specimens of medieval crafts-

80

manship and furnishing. It is true that the chronicles of the
Highlands are not encouraging reading to those who dislike
the thought of hot tempers and cold steel. ("Theology
tempered by murder" is my definition of much Scottish
history.) But such places as Crathie remind us that medieval
Scotland was not just a northern Barbary. It had, along
with its dirks and claymores, its close cultural links with
the craftsmen of Europe and a very high achievement
in the decorative arts. The Braes of Mar were remote,
but the standards of creative work in sixteenth-century
Scotland were high and could have spread from Aberdeen
up the broad and comparatively easy valley of the Dee to
Abergeldie.

Where the Geldie burn comes down from the forest there
begins an old route across the big hills to the glens of
Angus; here, too, was a valuable ford across the Dee and
access to the north as well. So Abergeldie became a
strategic position; it was accordingly fortified and equipped
with a moat which, together with the river, gave it almost an
island site. The moat has vanished and, inevitably, the
house suffered during stormy centuries the common fate of
castles when "broils root out the work of masonry." But
rebuilding followed ruination in the hopeful way of combatant man and the old tower is still there. Stirton described
it justly. "With its rounded angles, crow-stepped gables
and somewhat elaborately corbelled angle turret, it is a good
and picturesque example of a sixteenth-century manor house
in Aberdeenshire."[1]

The Gordons got possession of the Abergeldie lands,
previously a Mar property, by a grant from King James III
in 1487. Upper Deeside remained a centre of Roman

[1] *Crathie and Braemar*, p. 88.

Catholicism after the Reformation had reached Scotland, and the Old Religion is strong still in the Braes of Mar. There were bitter doctrinal contentions in and around the Gordon properties. In 1593 William Gordon of Abergeldie was denounced for not answering Privy Council charges concerning masses and " resetting of Priests and Papists." The family was not one to miss a war. Gordons of Abergeldie fought with Montrose and also with Dundee at Killiecrankie. In stern reply the victorious General Mackay later set up a garrison at the Castle in order to put discipline on Upper Deeside. The Gordons, however, created homes afresh. In 1715 Charles Gordon of Abergeldie built Birkhall, which was to become a favourite among the royal houses. Of this place there is more to be said later.

The Gordons, however, were not too proud to look beyond their own boundaries and to share the southward glance of Highland lairds at the end of the eighteenth century. The riches of the Industrial Revolution and the opportunities of commerce had then become magnetic to the impoverished chieftains of the glens. Business was no longer sordid in their eyes, an affair for Lowlanders and Englishmen only. This was exemplified in the case of Abergeldie. The fourteenth Laird, David Gordon, became a member of the firm of Gordon and Biddulph and married Anne Biddulph of Ledbury in the English midlands. These social changes brought alterations in education too; the dispatch of young Scots to the old English schools was now becoming the proper thing for the socially ambitious. At the end of the seventeenth century the Duke of Atholl did not hesitate to send his son, Lord George Murray, to the village school at Moulin near Pitlochry because it then had a notable dominie

in Adam Ferguson, later Minister at Crathie. David
Gordon sent his son Charles to Harrow where he became a
friend of Byron. Byron's ill-health took him to Deeside and
in one of his letters to David Gordon he speaks with rapture
of Abergeldie, " a most lovely place," as well as of dark-
frowning Lochnagar, the mountains above Mar Lodge,
and " the cataracts of Dee."

Queen Victoria and the Prince Consort, once established
at Balmoral, wished to buy Abergeldie, but the Gordons
were not selling. Nowadays the State, through its almost
omnipotent Civil Servants, grabs lands and houses as it
wishes and the wishes may outrun real needs; it serves
expropriation notices without mercy on owners and tenants
and gives them in the course of time such compensation as
it chooses, which may be almost nothing. Royalty, at least
during recent years, has not had these powers of seizure and
would be too humane to use them if it had. Hence Abergeldie remained a lease-hold: hence, too, the great forest of
Ballochbuie, to the west of Balmoral, known as " the
bonniest plaid in Scotland," remained in the Farquharsons'
hands until 1878, when it was purchased from that family
for nearly £100,000. The sale had been delayed for some
time, despite the known fact that the Queen had wanted to
buy it.

For many years Abergeldie, held on long lease though
not royally owned, played second to Balmoral as the
recipient of royalty. Queen Victoria's mother, the Duchess
of Kent, was in residence during the summers of 1850-1857.
After that her doctors forbade her to make the full journey
and she took her holiday in the South of Scotland. At the
time of her accession in 1837 the young Queen had to show
great courage and determination in resisting her mother's

desire to dominate or at least to bear a large part of the new responsibilities; but, once it had been made plain that Victoria and Victoria alone was the Queen, their relations became most affectionate. The Duchess's death (at Frogmore in 1861) was the first severe blow in that dreadful year which was to end with the loss of Albert, the Queen's utter desolation, and the prolonged mourning.

Mrs. Lindsay, who was much at the Castle in her youth, has left us a pleasant picture of Abergeldie's first tenant under the new leasehold. As a little girl she found the Duchess of Kent " a stout, comely, elderly lady whose face overflowed with kindliness and good humour, quietly dignified, yet with a gentle courtesy that set even a shy child at ease." The old lady was fond of her game of cards, Patience or Whist, fonder still of her piano and her dogs, especially a white poodle. She was happy in entertaining, and the dances for tenants and staff were spirited occasions with the local fiddlers in vigorous action. The Duchess always appeared dressed in an old-fashioned cap of lace and ribbons. On her death, the Prince of Wales took over the house and used it continually for his autumn stay in Scotland and for the entertainment of his shooting parties. When he was not there, there were other tenants including the ex-Empress Eugénie.

Abergeldie has all that an ancient castle should possess, from a ration of ghosts to a girdle of gardens. Its antiquity is proven by a large monolith on the riverside lawns: the Stone Age men had seen the advantage and amenity of its site. It has long been rich in trees. The Scottish countryside owes much to the " gean," the wild cherry, A. E. Housman's fairest of trees, which in the far north wears its white rather after Eastertide. The centre and north-east of

Scotland have been rich in poets who mostly sing of the hues
and humours of the land in the natural " speak " of its
people. Violet Jacob, Marion Angus and Helen Cruickshank,
as well as Charles Murray of Donside, have been excellent
in this kind, with Douglas Young of Dundee voicing a
wider scholarship as well. One usually finds the geans
flowering in the green Howe of the Mearns and in the
memories of the writers.

There is also a famous larch-tree. The Scottish larches,
so delicately green in May and sometimes made yet more
attractive by the antics of a red squirrel, are a constant
decoration of the lawns and grounds of the big houses. (The
monkey-tree, a foolish importation, is no less constant and
is certainly no ornament with its alien prickliness.) The
arrival of the larch is fairly recent; we owe it to a Duke of
Atholl who brought it from Norway and established a larch
plantation at Dunkeld. His visitors found the trees so
pleasant to the eye that they frequently asked for seedlings
to plant on their own estates. Thus the larch reached Invercauld, and, according to an anecdote recorded by Mrs.
Lindsay,[1] it took a prominent place in the *décor* of Abergeldie owing to a snapping up of unconsidered trifles. One
of the lairds of Invercauld asked the laird of Abergeldie
how he came by such a fine larch tree, outstripping his own
in size. The reply came, " It's just ane o' yours, Invercauld,
that I put in ma pouch lang syne "; poaching (or pouching)
is a craft with many sides to it in Scotland. The lifting of
seedlings, which was probably a novelty, was at least introduced with a high social background and with an honest
confession of the deed.

Another curiosity of old Abergeldie was its aerial cross-

---

[1] *Recollections of a Royal Parish*, p. 78.

river transport. This was provided by a cradle attached to a strong cable. Two persons could be carried over the Dee in this frightening conveyance, and people continued to risk the passage despite the occurrence of a fatal crash in earlier years: two victims who were being thus whisked across the river, then in high spate, fell in and were drowned: this was just after their wedding. The wretched couple were a gamekeeper called Willie Frankie and Barbara Brown, who was known as the Flower of Deeside. A chain foot-bridge ultimately took the place of the cradle, but the chance to imitate " the daring young man on the flying trapeze who flies through the air with the greatest of ease " continued to lure the adventurous young for some time despite the obvious risks. There is a superstition that the Dee, with its tendency to ferocious flooding after the melting of the Cairngorm snows or a particularly heavy and prolonged downpour of rain, is certain to kill three people a year.

> *Blood-thirsty Dee*
> *Each year needs three,*
> *But Bonny Don,*
> *She needs none.*

The great flood of 1829 was well remembered for its ravages and Queen Victoria was to be reminded of Dee's menace to the local children when one of the Rattray boys was drowned. Abergeldie's ghosts include a witch and assorted warners of bad news to come. But it has not, in fact, been an unlucky house.

The Abergeldie land ran some miles down the river to the eastward, passing the Bridge of Girnock where Prince Albert had a school built for the benefit of Deeside scholarship. Thereafter the Birkhall estate is reached and this charming house, though Mrs. Lindsay described it as too small for a royal residence, has been found very convenient in later years, and is regularly occupied by members of the Royal Family. Birkhall, with an estate of 6,500 acres, was bought from the Gordons for the expected benefit of the Prince of Wales during the lifetime of his father, but was sold back to the Queen in 1885.

The house was built by Charles Gordon in 1715, the year of the first Jacobite rising, and in 1746 it sheltered two refugees who had escaped southward to the Dee from Culloden. They were Oliphants of Gask. It is especially interesting to note that the endangered Oliphants took the names of Brown and " Whytt " (or White); this bears out the theory that the sudden appearance in and round the Highlands of non-Gaelic colour-names, Brown, Black, White, Gray and so on, may have been due to their useful-ness in providing cover for Highlanders who had " gone underground." (This point is discussed later on in con-nection with the origins of the Crathie Browns from whom came Queen Victoria's personal atendant, John Brown.) Mr. Stirton, in his volume on *Crathie and Braemar* has re-printed letters showing how the Oliphants, under their new and supposedly safe names, scattered their property in friendly houses, with the Macintoshs at Moy and Reats, and with other friends in Glen Clova. Most of it, however, was " delivered to Mrs. Gordon at Birkhall " including " a sute of Hyland Cloaths and Phylibeg," also " a pair of red ever-lasting britches." The Oliphants escaped to Sweden after six months of miserable hiding and Mrs. Gordon could write to Lady Gask: " I rec'd a letter from a gentleman, written from Gottenborg, who writes me, Mr. White and Mr. Brown is in very good health. I trust in Almighty God you'll have the pleasure of seeing them in triumph soon and I am with regard and esteem,

> Your ladyship's most humble servt.
>
> ELIZA GORDON "

Mistress Gordon's grammar was imperfect: but her courage and compassion were beyond criticism. For she was risking much in her service of those flying from the bitter persecution which followed Culloden. So the beautiful house of Birkhall, looking eastward over Glen Muick and set beside one of the roads leading up to Loch Muick, had its romantic history during the Hard Times in the Highlands. It has since served, as Abergeldie did for so long, to provide a convenient home for the royal relations who wanted a place of their own. One of its possessions is a large collection of " Spy " cartoons.

Soon after their leasing of Sir Robert Gordon's Balmoral, Queen Victoria discovered that, paradisal though it be, it could still lack sufficiency of solitude. Accordingly she determined that a cottage far up Glen Muick in the wilderness beyond Birkhall should be turned into a habitable shelter for herself and her company when the passion for still more privacy and for even more strenuous exploration was upon her. Hence the plenishing of the cottage, its enlargement with a wooden addition, and the further construction of another small house a few yards away. This outpost was called by the name of the burn which poured down from Lochnagar to join the River Muick; it was Altna-Guithasach. It was first occupied on August 30, 1849. No time had been wasted in establishing a further retreat from the retreat that was Balmoral. This " bothie " or " The Hut " as it was often called, provided, in the larger building, two sitting-rooms, bedroom and dressing-room for the Queen and the Prince, together with a small room for the Lady-in Waiting and one for her maid. The Queen's diary says nothing of a bathroom. The other section of " The Hut " was used by a small staff.

The Queen loved it. The eye met everywhere " real severe Highland scenery "; the loch in its variety of weathers looked noble or sinister; Muich (or Muick) signified, so she was informed, " Darkness or Sorrow." The modern visitor who drives up the road (a rough and narrow one, but not too difficult) on the other side of the glen, can see this region of the royal solace stretching from Birkhall away up to the great chasm filled by the waters of Loch Muick. He can hardly disagree with the adjective " severe " and, if the weather is not ruinous to the view and to physical comfort, the Queen's additional adjectives " solemn and striking " may strike him as adequate. It is a recess for those who like the bare bones of the earth rather than the prospect of Nature furred and plumed.

That first lodgment in the desolate deer-forest south of the Dee afforded great delight. (Readers unused to the Highlands must not think of a " deer-forest " as a tree-covered area. It will have trees only in the lower sections and by the sides of the burns; far the greater part of it is open, naked mountain-side and mountain-summit.) Albert, never one to waste a holiday hour, took lessons in Gaelic from the ghillies. The ghillies found boats and rowed the party about the loch with a net; seventy trout were caught in this way, a procedure which might nowadays be frowned upon by all anglers and certainly would find small approval in the Fly Fishers' Club. There was some scrambling in and out of boats and up the rough tracks. Appetites were thus sharpened, while the senses were gratified by so much of "the picturesque."

After dinner there was dummy whist with the Lady-in-Waiting. It is possible that the latter, Miss Caroline Dawson, had other views about the bliss of life in a bothie. Mrs. Lindsay, writing with personal experience of "The Hut" at Alt-na-Guithasach, described her vivid recollections of the insect life. The trout and the midges of Loch Muick were both, in her opinion, "superlative in their way." It was during an evening by the waters of Muick that one of the party described the origin of the Highland Fling as " a kilt and midges." To be Lady-in-Waiting in the early years of the Queen's Highland life meant a share, bravely borne, in the ardours and endurances of the Expeditions. There were also other discomforts to be faced, even when the railway carried the Royal Train right up to Ballater. Sir Malcolm Barclay-Harvey in an article[1] on Royal Train Journeys to Deeside, described some of the difficulties:

"During the whole of Queen Victoria's reign, vestibule connections between the carriages making up the Royal Train were not allowed. This caused much discomfort to the ladies and others attending Her Majesty. It not infrequently happened that their services in the Royal Coach were dispensed with at some remote spot such as Beattock Summit, where no platform existed. As steps were only provided for the Royal Coach, the difficulties experienced by those ladies who had to regain their own compartments by climbing up from the ground with only carriage footboards to help can be imagined."

So sojourns at " The Hut " may have been comparatively

[1] The Scottish Annual—Braemar Gathering, 1954.

luxurious. There were harder trials to come on the Great Expeditions.

The fascination exercised by this area on the Queen was exemplified later in the same year by her resolve to explore a still more remote loch which lies, at a height of over 2,000 feet, away up behind Loch Muick and between the enclosing massiveness of Broad Cairn and Lochnagar. This was the Dubh or Dhu Loch, the Black Lake or Tarn. " The Hut " was useful for occupation during this expedition which ranged across some very rough country behind it to the far-flung loch surrounded by precipitous rocks. The journey involved some rough riding on the ponies: bogs had to be traversed and the Queen found that her mount, one supplied by Colonel Gordon, was broken-winded and " struggled very much in the soft ground, which was very disagreeable." The Lady-in-Waiting this time was Lady Douro, subsequently Duchess of Wellington; her opinions of the hard way to Loch Dubh are not quoted, but she certainly agreed with the Queen on one point. When the men were trying to end the outing by rowing them down Loch Muick in a storm and making no progress against the wind, the ladies decided that it would be much better to seek dry land, however rough. And very rough it was on a stony and narrow path with a sharp drop to the loch. " The Hut " was safely reached at last, after all the difficulties and adventures which, in the Queen's view, were " always very pleasant to look back upon." Lady Douro, called upon for dummy whist at the end of all this, might have preferred a speedier retirement. Were her memories as happy as those of the then all-enduring and indefatigable Queen? It must be remembered, when the Highland expeditions are in consideration, that she had recently given birth to five children within nine years. But still the roughest ways and loneliest peaks were no less magnetic than " dear Balmoral " itself.

After the death of the Prince Consort, " The Hut " could be used for a pause or a picnic; but it seemed intolerable to the widow to sleep yet again in the little shelter of their joint creation, the shelter where so much happiness had been found. Yet Loch Muick seemed to possess an irresistible fascination for the Queen; if she could not bring herself to spend waterside nights at Alt-na-Guithasach, then she must build again.

The site chosen was at the remote end of the Loch, where the Glasalt burn runs in from the White Mounth. Here was built the Glasalt Shiel with a few sheltering trees and a little wooded promontory running out into the water. It was a rather less diminutive version of the earlier hut, with the addition of good stables and a keeper's cottage. The Queen had only a sitting-room, bedroom and maid's room on the ground floor, opposite the dining-room and kitchen. The Lady-in-Waiting and guest, if any, were on the upper floor where there were three rooms for John Brown, the cook, and another servant.

The house-warming—or " fire-kindling "—took place on 1st October, 1868, nineteen years after the opening of " The Hut " at Alt-na-Guithasach. All the servants and a single policeman, who only came up to do night duty, joined in. There were five " animated reels," after the first of which whisky-toddy was brought round. The " good Grant " made a welcoming speech on behalf of the natives of these wilds and John Brown begged the Queen to partake of the whisky. The dance lasted till after eleven, but the men went on singing in the servants' room, " all very happy." The

Queen said that she was not disturbed, because " the little passage near my room shuts off everything." This suggests a kindly understatement. She must, in a comparatively small house, have heard quite a good deal, passage or no passage; passages are not stone walls nor was the Glasalt Shiel proofed against sound. The Queen could be compassionately deaf when her favourite ghillies, and especially John Brown, well established in favour by this time, were indulging in whisky and high spirits.

But it was inevitably a sad occasion. " I was alone . . . I thought of the happy past and of my darling husband whom I fancied I must see and who always wished to build here, in this favourite wild spot, quite in amidst the hills. At Alt-na-Guithasach I could not have lived alone now. It is far better to have built a totally new house; but then the sad thought struck me that it was the first *Widow's house*, not built by him or hallowed by his memory. But I am sure his blessing does rest on it and on those who live in it."[1]

Those who choose to sneer at the *Journals* can do so. They were written without art; they poured out the simplest essence of mourning amid the descriptions of mountain-rapture. They are now the required reading for all who journey up Glen Muick, past the serenity of Birkhall to " The Hut " and the second Shiel beside the loch of sadness and on the way to the Black Loch beneath the White Mounth that is snow-capped before autumn is out. In *More Leaves* the shadows are always round the corner, and the clouds come down upon the feelings as surely as the storms roll down from Lochnagar.

Then, with the fire duly kindled in Glasalt, back went the Queen to Balmoral and the pleasures of the simple,

[1] *More Leaves from the Journal*, p. 107.

social round: there was the spectacle of the sheep being "juiced" "in a large sort of trough filled with liquid tobacco and soap"; there were the village "kirstnins" (christenings), with toddy and cakes; there was the comforting of the old and dying Mrs. Grant, a friend for twenty-one years; there were the laughter and the lamentations of the Crathie folk. And then the always painful journey south, lightened only by the thoughts of next year's return.

Two years later the shores of Loch Muick were to be the scene of a "dander" which had results similar to those of Prince Frederick's walk with "Vicky" up the Girnoch glen. On an October day, Princess Louise took the track from the Glasalt Shiel away up to the Dhu Loch with the Marquis of Lorne. Another daughter was requested in marriage and gave her consent. So did the Queen.

The estates had been a constant care of Prince Albert and were naturally a care of the Queen; surely nothing could be more false or cruel than the suggestion that the attitude of the "Clearance" landlords was a phase of Balmorality. So far from there being evictions in the interests of sport, there was encouragement to settle and stay on the Balmoral lands. Dr. Robertson was in charge of estate affairs for thirty-three years and he was universally popular with the tenants as well as esteemed by his employers. He was appointed Commissioner in Scotland for the Queen on the recommendation of Lord Aberdeen. Previously he had been the Crathie doctor with a practice which took him on many a long, rough journey on horseback; he thus knew almost every house and was not a stranger brought in to regulate the lives and work of people he did not understand.

In a book on *The Prince Consort's Farms*, J. C. Morton described the care shown by the new owners of Balmoral:

"Comfortable cottages have replaced the former miserable dwellings; farm offices, according to the size of the farms, have been erected; money has been advanced for the draining, trenching, and improvement of waste land; new roads have been opened up and old ones repaired; fences have been renewed and upwards of one thousand acres of unreclaimable land planted. But it was not to agricultural improvements alone that His Royal Highness's attention was directed; he saw the advantage of encouraging tradesmen and labourers of good character to settle upon his estates. Houses and gardens, with a croft where it could be conveniently added, were provided at a moderate rent, and the extensive works thus undertaken were carried on over a series of years so as to give constant employment."

There was a library made available to all. Doubtless the anti-Balmoralists will seize upon the phrase "of good character" to suggest that character-tests were imposed. But what landlord wants bad characters for tenants? There is no discoverable evidence that the estates were managed in any high-handed way with a rigid ethic imposed on those working on the land or in their various trades. (The local Elders of the Kirk were busy enough with this kind of imposition.) The fact that John Brown, with his known frailties, was promoted to a very high and confidential position does not suggest that the régime was of too austere a kind. The Highlanders had won a regard which was liberal in its outlook as well as cordial in its temper.

Queen Victoria's happy curiosity about the Highlands led her to extensive and arduous travels by carriage, on pony, and, where necessary, on foot. The houses, whether Castle or Shiel, were used as bases for the Great Expeditions which began in 1860 and were continued in 1861. During the single day of September 6, 1860, the Queen, with the Prince, Lady Churchill and General Grey, left Balmoral at eight in the morning in "the sociable" and drove to Braemar and up to the Linn of Dee. Here, where carriage-travel became impossible, they took ponies and rode by moorland track to the Geldie burn. The ground was so boggy and soft that the ponies could not carry riders and there had to be dismountings and splashy walkings. And so, round the southern bastion of the Cairngorms, they worked their way into Glen Feshie, which the Queen spelt as Glen Fishie; here they lunched at two. Then they rode another twelve rough miles to a somewhat hazardous ferry over the Spey. "So far we had gone forty miles, at least twenty on horseback."

It was six in the evening before they reached a carriage-road where there was a conveyance waiting—the Expeditions must have demanded some staff-work—and then came a three-hours' drive to Granton. They were travelling as "Lord and Lady Churchill and Party" and may or may not have been recognised. Their lodging was an inn which provided a small room with a four-poster for the Queen and her husband. They had the inn-dinner (a good one) served by the maid of the house and they got to bed by half-past eleven.

On the following day they rose early, breakfasted "on tea, bread and butter, and excellent porridge," and travelled to Tomintoul through mist and rain. It is a heavy, uphill journey, as modern motorists with a good road are aware; for horse traffic it was desperately slow motion—fourteen miles took four hours. Tomintoul can now seem, despite its

height and loneliness, a place of some amenity; to Queen
Victoria it was far from attractive. But it must be remembered in its defence that she had arrived after a long, wet,
and lumbering drive. After lunch there the carriages were
left and pony-riding became essential. They thus covered
the next eight miles up Glen Avon to Inchory and on to
Loch Builg. Here the staff-work had arranged for carriages
to be ready and it was possible to drive down Glen Gairn
to Balmoral, which was reached at half-past seven.

It is difficult, in these days of forty miles an hour on good
Highland roads and of Landrover travel across the forest
tracks, to realise what a strain this circuit of the Cairngorms
in two days involved on a woman who was no longer a girl
but the mother of a large family. Yet it was held to be " a
delightful, successful expedition " with Lady Churchill
" thoroughly amiable, cheerful and ready to do everything."
Those who have covered this bit of country in the hard,
pedestrian way will know what it all meant. The Queen
ended her entranced description with a tribute to the ponies
and congratulations to everybody except herself. Readers
of the *Journal* and of its record of the Expeditions should
follow them on a map as well as visualise the conditions of
travel at the time. The first day's journey from Balmoral
to Granton cannot have been less than seventy miles.

The year of 1860 was a blank one in the *Journals*. The
birth of another child, the boy who was to be Arthur, Duke
of Connaught, the seventh of nine born in seventeen years,
meant a more stationary holiday. But in 1861 the Expedi-
tionary Fever rose to its height. Between 20th September
and 16th October the country was covered from Fettercairn
in the east to Loch Avon in the north and Blair Atholl in
the west. The first trip took them over the steep mountain-

barrier to the south of Deeside and involved a climb to 3,200 feet on Mount Keen. This was included in a day's travel of forty miles, with forty-two more on the following day.

The greatest excursion of all was that westward to the main Highland road with a ride of fifteen miles followed by a drive of twenty-nine miles through Bridge of Carr, Kingussie, and Newtonmore to the inn at Dalwhinnie, where the supper was " only tea, two miserable starved Highland chickens with no potatoes, no pudding and no fun." (Poor staff-work this time!) However, the next morning was fine and the long drive to Blair Atholl and coffee with the Duke was enjoyed. Then came the return to Braemar by way of Glen Tilt, a superb journey, as many a walker knows, but a very rough and a very long one. Carriages could be taken for the eight miles up to Forest Lodge and then ponies were mounted and an hour's riding followed; a picnic lunch was taken at three. There were pipers to raise the travellers' spirits and there was rain to depress them. There was quite a struggle to get across the ford of the rain-swollen Tarff and there were precipitous bits of the path to be scrambled over on foot. At the borders of Inverness and Aberdeenshire the Duke of Atholl produced whisky, proposed the Queen's health, and set the Highlanders cheering her on her way. The Bainoch Lodge —now Bynack on the Ordnance maps—was reached just before six and a welcome tea provided by Lady Fife. The Duke of Atholl then turned back for the long dark ride home to Blair on this difficult track; the waiting carriages did the twenty miles back to Balmoral at a good pace. The royal party were home by a quarter past eight.

Once more the record was rapturous, " The pleasantest

and most enjoyable expedition I ever made." Since the
death of the Duchess of Kent there had been no such
alleviation of sorrow. They had travelled 119 miles in two
days, including the crossing of the Glen Tilt water, on pony
and on foot. " Did not feel tired," wrote the Queen, adding:
" We ladies did not dress and dined *en famille*." But even
that was not enough of the Paradise; after dinner the
evening was spent " looking at maps of the Highlands."

The ghillies who walked at the ponies' heads when the
ground was very slippery or rugged may well have felt more
fatigued. And what of Lady Churchill and the Prince?
What is surprising is the concentration of the travel. It
would have been easy and agreeable to stop a night at Blair
Atholl with such great friends as the Duke and Duchess
instead of hammering on at Glen Tilt and so making a two-
day job of what might more agreeably have been a three- or
even a four-day Expedition. It is possible that Prince
Albert, by so gladly acquiescing in these long treks through
all weathers, began the weakening of his constitution which
was to prove so rapidly fatal. He died within two months
of the last Great Expedition. After the return to London,
there had been worry about the Prince of Wales and his
conduct at Cambridge, a hurried visit to the University to
see the errant son, followed by a rash outing, when he was
plainly ill, to watch the Queen review the Eton Volunteers.
There was, moreover, the nervous strain caused by the risk
of war with the American Government over the Trent affair.
The Prince Consort's modification of a too petulant Foreign
Office dispatch was prudent and saved the situation. His
last act of policy was of great benefit to the world. But,
when he minuted the dispatch, his brain was driving a
weakened hand. He could hold his own with Lord

Palmerston, but he could hardly hold his pen. "Gastric fever" set in—typhoid to us. The venerable doctors of the Household gathered round and achieved little. He walked in his sleep. His mind wandered and just before midnight on 14th December he moaned indistinctly to the Queen that he grieved so much to leave so good a wife and died. Lord Clarendon said of the aged and august medicos who attended him, "They are not fit to attend a sick cat." He would surely not have died with modern attention.

So "The Hut" of Alt-na-Guithasach beside Loch Muick was no more occupied on summer nights and the Widow's House was erected, seven years later, at Glasalt. The loch was too dear to be deserted. But there had to be a refuge from memories of the shared Expedition which had passed "The Hut" on the way from Balmoral over the mountain barrier to the southward and into the glens of Angus, a refuge, also, from recollection of the shorter, one-day scrambles away up to the Loch Dhu, the Black Tarn, lying grim between the grimmer shoulders of Cairn Bannoch and the White Mounth. So the Glasalt Shiel was at once the balm of a sore mind and a base for journeys still to be made; there were the sons and daughters to possess it, if they chose. Courtship, more often associated with green thoughts in green shades, was pursued in this bare and lofty wilderness. Love in a Cold Climate is a title to fit the wooing of Princess Louise by the Marquis of Lorne. This Princess was the only one of Queen Victoria's children to marry into Scotland and the proposal was fitly made by the Duke of Argyll's heir in a scene so essentially Highland as the path to Loch Dhu.

CHAPTER FIVE

Stag Parties

THE Braes of Mar, westerly neighbours to the Balmoral lands, were a traditional scene of Scottish hunting and shooting. These pursuits were at one time more calculated to fill the larder than to challenge the muscularity, the endurance, and the accuracy of finger and of eye possessed by the partakers of the exercise. The exercise, as carried out on the flanks of the Cairngorms, whether on the Aberdeenshire or the Perthshire side, at one time had the size of a military operation.

In 1563 Queen Mary " took the sport of hunting the deer in the Forest of Mar and Atholl," and so was one of Queen Victoria's predecessors in the enjoyment of this region and in spectatorship of its sports. On this occasion two thousand Highlanders were summoned to spend several weeks in herding the stags to the amount of two thousand, beside roes, does, and other game. At one time this enormous host of stags appears to have become annoyed with the pro-ceedings; its members charged their beaters, " who knew well the power of this phalanx," and knew also that safety lay only in prostration. They fell flat on the heath and allowed the deer to run over them; " but it did not save them from being wounded and it was announced to the

Queen that two or three had been trampled to death." A few casualties of this kind appear to have caused no worry; a flanking movement managed to get the stampeding stags back into their proper course and ultimately into the corner of the glen appointed for the slaughter. Then "the stag-hounds of the Queen and of the nobility were loosed, three hundred and sixty deer were killed, five wolves and some roes." The Queen and her party then went off down Glen Tilt to Blair Atholl, "delighted with the sport." Presumably there were some pensions allotted to the widows of those who fell flat and fell for ever.

There is no mention of firearms in this rather hazy and improbable account of Queen Mary's sporting tour. But a few years after that, according to an early historian and raconteur of deer-stalking, William Scrope, author of *Days of Deer-Stalking in the Forest of Atholl* (1847), a blunderbuss was used in Sutherland by Angus Baillie of Uppat, a notable pioneer. Scrope surmised that this article was taken from the wreck of a Spanish Armada galleon which was cast on the shores of Scotland. However that may be, we have the evidence of Taylor, the English Water Poet who attended a similar battue, that early in the seventeenth century the harquebus, as well as bows and arrows, was employed in the deer-hunt. This weapon must have been that described by Scrope as "a very rude gun, having the barrel attached to the stock by iron hoops."

In the sixteenth century there was no feeling that the quarry should be given a fair chance of escape. Queen Elizabeth had no qualms about practising her archery on deer securely corralled in front of her, and that with music and a little masquerade for embellishment; at Cowdray, in Sussex, in August, 1593, there was a "delicate bowrie prepared, under which Her Highness's musicians were placed; a crossbow, by a nymph with a sweet song, was delivered into her hands to shoot at the deer; about some thirty were put into a paddock, of which number she killed three or four and the Countess of Kildare one." Shakespeare understood that kind of queenly dalliance with carnage and introduced just such a piece of parkland archery when the King of Navarre entertained the Princess of France in *Love's Labour's Lost*. Duke Theseus, however, and his Hippolyta in *A Midsummer Night's Dream* were more strenuous in the chase. They really followed hounds instead of potting deer driven to a paddock. " We will, fair queen, up to the mountain's top." The young Queen Victoria, so assiduous in her bagging of the peaks, would have appreciated that line with its early proclamation of " Excelsior " as proper to the exercise of hunting.

With the arrival of firearms there seems to have been increasing enthusiasm in the Braes of Mar for a grand concourse of the gentry and a stag-party *de luxe*. The chiefs of the Highland Clans assembled in August on the upper waters of the Dee and gave six weeks to effecting a considerable carnage among the birds and herds driven down from the Cairngorms. If the account left by the London rhymer and pamphleteer, John Taylor, is at all accurate their huge raids upon the fauna would hardly be described nowadays in terms of sport. (Taylor expressly avowed his accuracy, which some may regard as cause for suspicion. Why be so touchy about one's good name for truth-telling?) In this concourse of slaying and feasting the owners and the tenants of the Invercauld and Balmoral estates would be natural participants. The numbers engaged seem to be, as in the case of Queen Mary's day with the hounds,

enormous; they seem incredible if we consider the population of these parts nowadays. Taylor related that there were
" fourteen or fifteen hundred men in our camp " and that
this was victualled by " Falconers, Fowlers, Fishers, and
my Lord's tenants and purveyors."

The record left by Taylor throws so much light on the
state of the Highlands and especially of Upper Deeside in
the early seventeenth century, that it is worth studying in
some detail. His fore-page, to some extent the equivalent
of the modern " blurb," describes himself and his adventure
thus:

THE PENNYLES PILGRIMAGE,

or
The money-leffe perambulation
of John Taylor, Alias
the Kings Majesties
Water-Poet.

HOW HE TRAVELLED ON FOOT
from London to Edenborough in Scotland, not carrying
any Money to or fro, neither Begging, Borrowing, or
Asking Meate, drinke or Lodging.

With his Description of his Entertainment

in all places of his Iourney, and a true Report of the
vnmatchable Hunting in the Brea of Marre and
Badenoch in Scotland.

With other Obferuations, fome ferious and worthy
of Memory, and fome merry and not hurtfull to be
Remembred.

Lastly that (which is rare in a Trauailer) all is True.

104

LONDON
Printed by Edw: Allde, at the charges of the Author.
1618.

Taylor may have walked much of the way, as Ben Jonson was doing at the same time on his visit to Drummond of Hawthornden, but he had a gelded nag to carry his " provant " (provender) when he left the Bell Inn, Aldersgate, on 14th July, 1618. The condition of the journey was that he should not ask for hospitality, but he obviously had many valuable introductions; much hospitality was arranged in advance and he was liberally entertained. This was partly because he could style himself the poet of the King's Majesty and so belonged in some way to the Royal House-hold (he dedicated his book on return to the King's favourite, George Villiers, Marquis of Buckingham) and partly because a Londoner arriving in some of the towns through which he passed was such a rarity that entertainment was spontaneously offered. At the same time he had good larder-luggage on the nag's back:

> " *There in my knapsack (to pay hunter's fees),*
> *I had good bacon, biscuit, neat's tongue, cheese,*
> *With roses, barberries, of each conserves,*
> *And mithridate, that vigorous health preserves:* "

He also had oil, vinegar and brandy in his stock as he travelled north by the western route, passing Islington, Whetstone, Dunstable and Daventry, where he ran into a solitary example of bad manners:

> " *They drank of my beer, that to me was given*
> *But gave me not a drop to make odd even.*"

However, he subsequently apologised to the innkeeper for the rude remarks he passed on him. So by way of Coventry, Lichfield, Stone, Newcastle-under-Lyme, to Adlington, near Macclesfield, where he was entertained by the historic family of Leigh. Next he enjoyed the rich hospitality of Mr. Edmund Prestwich in Manchester, two nights and a day, and had a wash and shave from his host's private barber. Taylor devotes pages to Mancunian kindliness at the table and bounty of wardrobe too:

> " *Nothing they thought too heavy or too hot,*
> *Can followed can and pot succeeded pot . . .*
> *And these eight several sorts of ale we had*
> *All able to make one stark drunk or mad. . . .*
> *And further to express their boundless loves*
> *They saw I wanted, and they gave me, gloves.*"

Preston, Sedbergh, Penrith and Carlisle were passed and Scotland entered. Edinburgh, by way of Moffat, was reached at two in the afternoon on 13th August. By this time the water-poet, no water-drinker, described himself, after a month on the road, as " hobbling." One is not surprised.

In the Scottish capital he found " entertainment beyond my expectation or merit," and a general condition of satisfaction. " Every night before I went to bed, if any man had asked me a civil question, all the wit in my head could not have made him a sober answer."

Fife was explored, especially " the most admirable coal mines," submarine as well as underground, at Culross; moving westward to Stirling and back eastward to Perth, he learned that the Earl of Mar and Sir William Murray of Abercairnie " were gone to the great hunting in the Brae

of Mar, but if I made to ask, I might find them at Brechin."
So he hurried, with a guide, to Brechin and found his hosts
" gone thence four days." There was nothing for it but a
strenuous pursuit across the Eastern Grampians, if the
water-poet was to be in at the deer-slaughter amid the Braes
of Mar.

Another guide led him up Glen Esk to Edzell. Taylor
has muddled his memories here, for he writes of fearsome
Highland country between Brechin and Edzell. The route
there must have been comparatively gentle: the severities
were yet to come. In the Laird of Edzell's land, he was given
lodging in an " Irish house." (The folks there had very
little English and Taylor always alluded to Gaelic as Irish.)
The insect-life therein was also alien. " In bed," he says,
" I was so stung with Irish musquitoes, a creature that hath
six legs and lives like a monster altogether upon man's flesh ;
they do inhabit and breed most in sluttish houses and this
house was none of the cleanest: the beast is much like a
louse in England, both in shape and nature." However, he
records that this was his only lousy bed in all his Scottish
travels and " with a shift that I had I shifted off my cannibals
and was never more troubled with them."

Then came his introduction to the genuinely big hills.
" The next day I travelled over an exceedingly high mountain called Mount Skene," where he met with the common
Highland experience of finding the Glen very warm and the
Ben very cold. On the summit of this Mount Skene, which
is now called Keen, his teeth chattered " like Virginals'
jacks " (i.e. piano-keys). Worse still, " a familiar mist
embraced me round and the old proverb of a Scottish mist
was verified in wetting me to the skin." It took him and his

guide four hours to cover six miles, as they fought on through
" stones, bogs, quagmires and long heath."

Yet by night he had reached the " Brae of Mar, which
is a large county." Presumably he did actually stop in or
near the Castleton of Kindrochit, later known as Braemar.
This was good going for the man who had recently hobbled
into Edinburgh and was, by profession, more waterman than
pedestrian. The distance from what is now Edzell to Loch
Lee at the top of Glen Esk is sixteen miles. Presuming that
his guide took him over the flank of Mount Skene (or
Keen), thus saving 800 feet by avoiding the summit (3,077
feet), they would have had seven miles of hard going before
they reached this highest point and could begin to drop
down into Glen Muick.

The enormous mass of Lochnagar and White Mounth
stood between them and Braemar, involving gruelling
climbs that could hardly have been tried by men who had
gone so far already. They must either have taken the track
beside the river Muick which leads to Ballater, or forced
their way round Conichcraig and descended to Abergeldie
and Balmoral. The latter route is the rougher, but shorter.
But even that meant a fifteen-mile scramble from the flanks
of Mount Skene. If Taylor really did get from the lands
of Edzell to Braemar in a day, even aided by a guide and a
pony, with four hours devoted to covering six miles and
with a drenching included, he was worthy to be a Highland
ghillie of the best. Whichever route he finally took, by
Ballater and up the ancient road (or track) to Braemar, or
down Glen Gelder to Abergeldie, he must have passed the
site of Balmoral.

If he covered this immense distance, even with what he
calls " extreme travel ", his guide must have found him a

new pony when he reached Deeside at one village or another. If, at the end of the long day, he rode past Crathie he may have paused to look across the river to the old estate of the Gordons which passed to the Farquharsons and ultimately to Britain's Royal Family. However tangled the forest may have been at the time, there would be some exquisite views reaching up in the summer twilight to the summit of Lochnagar. But we can reasonably assume that the Londoner was by now too weary for much sightseeing and longed only for a long drink, a large meal, and a bed free from " Irish musquitoes."

As the company which he was now to meet was of a most exalted order and his lodging was in the house of the Lord of Mar, he escaped, as he explained, further molestation, and was able to join what he called " the sport " in the soaring wilderness of Upper Deeside. The heights astonished the man from the Thames. They made the little knobs of his southern acquaintance, " Shooter's Hill," " Gad's Hill," " Highgate Hill " and " Hampstead Hill " seem " but mole-hills in comparison or like a liver or a gizard under a capon's wing, in respect of the altitude of their tops or the perpendicularity of their bottoms." Even in August he saw Ben Avon, most easterly of the Cairngorm mass, with " a furred mist upon his snowy head instead of a nightcap "; the snow he found to be constant on the summits.

Thus impressed, he joined a party of the best blood in Scotland, " John Erskine, Earl of Mar, James Stewart, Earl of Murray, George Gordon, Earl of Enzie, son and heir to the Marquess of Huntly, and others with their Countesses." (There was no question of the ladies staying quietly with their needlework.) There were a hundred of other Knights and Esquires, a troop of gentry as large, and perhaps as voracious, as that swarm of lordly locusts which accompanied King Lear, to the great ruin of his daughters' larders and to the great indignation of those ladies themselves. A Deeside Shooting Party in 1618 was no small matter: the terrain was already famous for what the English papers used to describe every August as " the rush to the moors." With " the Countesses " attending, there was perfect material for the Press Photographers and the group picture in the glossy weeklies; but the Deeside cameras were two and a half centuries away.

As far as the men were concerned, the " Tailor and Cutter " would have lacked copy, for Taylor reports the austerity and similarity of the Gent's Sporting Outfit of the day. The Countesses, no doubt, were not to be thus levelled into a dull unity of attire and would have given matter to the gossips. But of the Lords, Taylor writes: " all and every man in general in one habit, as if Lycurgus had been there and made laws of equality." The habit is described in detail, beginning at ground level:

" Their habit is shoes with but one sole apiece; stockings (which they call short hose) made of a warm stuff of divers colours, which they call tartan: as for breeches, many of them nor their forefathers, never wore any, but a jerkin of the same stuff that their hose is of, their garters being bands or wreaths of hay or straw, with a plaid about their shoulders, which is a mantle of divers colours, of much finer and lighter stuff than their hose, with blue flat caps on their heads, a handkerchief knit with two knots about their neck; and thus are they attired."

This costume appears to have been obligatory. There was some democratic pressure, indeed the menace of a strike, to

enforce it. If the Lairds did not conform, then the ghillies
" will disdain to hunt or willingly bring in their dogs; but
if men be kind to them and be in this habit, then are they
conquered with kindness and the sport will be plentiful.
That was the reason that I found so many noblemen and
gentlemen in these shapes (costumes)." The good Lord of
Mar saw to it that his London guest was also put into the
" shape " and became thus trouserless, blue-capped, and
tartan-hosed. Having obeyed the rules, the Englishman was
permitted, like any of the lordly ones, to go up into the hills.
Students of the ancient clan-customs of Scotland usually
emphasise the large amount of democratic equality enjoyed
under a paternal Chieftain; Taylor's notes on the ghillies'
aversion to sartorial class-distinction are useful evidence on
their side.

After being shown the local sights (or sight), the ruins of
Kindrochit Castle, the Waterman was introduced to
Aberdeenshire in good earnest; he may in his sporting tour
have entered Banff as well. For he was to be twelve days
without seeing house, cornfield or habitation and he began
to doubt whether he would ever see civilisation again. This
was no single-day excursion to the forest or the grouse-moor
with Landrover cars to help; the whole cavalcade went out,
as it were, on safari. They carried, for armament, " long
bows and forked arrows, swords and targets, harquebusses,
muskets, dirks and Lochaber axes." Although Taylor wrote
of his isolation from housing, he does seem to have had a
roof over his head at one time in the expedition. For just
as Queen Victoria built her bothies on Loch Muick and
elsewhere in order to save return to Balmoral every night,
so the Earls of Mar had their Lonchards or primitive
shooting-boxes; Taylor was billeted in that of " my good

Lord Erskine." There may have been some rough bedding in a Lonchard, but there was no lack of food and drink in the larder, and the open-air kitchen, set on the side of a bank, was a scene of furious activity. Not only did the day's " bag " provide game, but there were the farmyard meats and fowls as well. The Londoner describes with some gusto:

". . . many spits turning and winding, with great variety of cheer: as venison baked, sodden, roast, and stewed beef, mutton, goats, kid, hares, fresh salmon, pigeons, hens, capons, chickens, partridge, moor-coots, heath-cocks, caper-cailzies, and termagants (ptarmigans); good ale, sack, white, and claret, tent (or Alicante), with most potent Aquavitae."

The epoch of the simple flask and of the sandwich had not yet come.

The method of the hunting and shooting of the deer, which Taylor was later to describe in fond remembrance as " unmatchable," was nothing so strenuous as walking up or stalking. The procedure was a huge circular drive by the hundreds of beaters who brought whole herds down to an appointed spot where the dispatch of the animals by men thus armed was simple enough. The scouts or beaters were called Tinchels. The Tinchels, numbering on this occasion five or six hundred, rose early while the Lairds were sleeping the sleep of the well-dined, and went off to the big hills to surround and assemble the deer in herds which might contain as many as three or four hundred. The herds were then driven to the place of slaughter where " the guns " (or " the bows ") were waiting. Taylor surmises that some of the deer fell on the way since " the Tinchel-men do lick their own fingers, that is, like cooks, partake of the feast before it is served." The rest of the driven beasts in great multitude, " their heads making a show like a wood " on the surrounding hills, were urged into the valley where two hundred strong Irish greyhounds were ready for them. So were the nobility and gentry with the bows, the harque-busses, and the daggers. Taylor saw eighty deer killed within two hours. The venison was distributed, as the hunting outfit was worn, in an equalitarian way: the Tinchels had plenty to drag home.

If by the word sport we imply an effort on the part of the killer in order to match his skill and his endurance with the killed, that old hunting and shooting in the Braes of Mar was far from sporting. On the other hand, with so much and such speedy slaughter, there may have been less actual cruelty than when incompetent marksmen are out on the hills or town-bred poachers are seeking saleable meat and do as much wounding as killing. Taylor, however, had no qualms, and saluted his hosts with a brace of sonnets in gratitude for his share in " the Caledonian annual peaceful war." He decided that " the sport is manly " since,

> " *None bleed but beasts*
> *And last the victor on the vanquished feasts.*"

The man from the Thames proclaimed his happy surrender to the charms of Deeside and its mountains:

> " *Then let who list delight in vales below,*
> *Sky-kissing mountains pleasure are for me.*"

After some gloating over the size of the bag, fourscore fat deer dispatched in two hours, he concluded, with more rapture than logic :

" Lowland, your sports are low as is your seat,
The Highland games and minds are high and great."

After the carnage and the return to the Lonchard, " there
was such baking, boiling, roasting and stewing as if Cook
Ruffian had been there to have scalded the devil in his
feathers." The honoured Englishman was then taken on
to further and similar " sport " in Badenoch; he was a
guest at Ruthven and Balloch Castle (later called Castle
Grant). Taylor seems to have been a considerable snob, for
he lists his fellow-guests as another kind of " bag." At
Balloch he lived four days with four Earls, one Lord, and
divers Knights and Gentlemen, all of whom had their own
footmen. The hospitality was so intense that the readily
absorbent Waterman was finally driven, at least for a while,
to what is known as the water-wagon :

> " . . . at every meal four long tables furnished with all
> varieties: our first and second course being three score
> dishes at one board; and after that always a banquet:
> and there if I had not forsworn wine till I came to
> Edinburgh I think I had there drunk my last."

Oft-sworn repentance rarely endures. Once free of his
headaches and back in Edinburgh, it was easy for Taylor
to be a back-slider. During his return journey he met Ben
Jonson at Leith and was given a piece of gold of two and
twenty shillings by the generous Ben " to drink his health
in England." But the money appears to have been spent
by Taylor over " the social glass " in Edinburgh, which
city he says he left, as he had entered it, penniless. And so
we may take leave of him, acknowledging with thanks his
vivid picture of what the sporting life and its " unmatchable

hunting " meant in this part of the Highlands during the early years of the seventeenth century. If the Earl of Mar and his associates are to be censured for shooting at a mass of driven and cornered stags with no hope of escape, instead of enduring the rigours and displaying the skill of a long " stalk," they have at least some excuse in the speed of the execution. The man who shoots at a sitting pheasant, traditionally the action of an ignorant townee, is at least fairly certain to hit it, whereas the " sportsman " who frightens the bird into flight before he will fire may be more likely to wound it and see it flutter off to a slow death. But it is unlikely that the Earl and his guests, including the vagrant Londoner, gave any thought to the ethics or humanities when they went forth in August " wi' six hundred tinchels and a' and a' " to thin the huge herds in the corries of Lochnagar or the Cairngorms and to set the cooks working overtime.

The game reserves of the Braemar and Balmoral region were undiminished when Thomas Pennant toured Scotland in 1769. The hunting meetings of the nobility may have declined after the disaster of Culloden and the harrying and dispersion of the clansmen. Such gatherings would, with reason, be held dangerous by the House of Hanover since it was during one of them that the first move was made from sport to insurrection. Many of the assembled sportsmen, raising the standard of revolt at Braemar in 1715, went out to fight a greater enemy than the Tinchel-driven stags. Pennant in his book *A Tour in Scotland* speaks of the " unmatchable hunting " which Taylor had enjoyed, as a thing of " old times." Braemar he found romantic and " unnecessarily occupied " by English troops. (These marched into Braemar after " the '45 " and remained for many years.) He had come to Deeside the hard way, threading the track up Glen Tilt; there he found " the road the most dangerous and most horrible I have ever travelled." It was a hard route—and still is—but he showed both bad temper and bad taste by calling the exquisite tumble of the Tilt " this dreary stream." He then worked round the bastion of the Cairngorms; accordingly his observations on the wild life would be made at first hand as well as on local information. He reported vast abundance of red deer, roe-deer and black game. " The tops of the hills swarmed with grouse and ptarmigans." Green plover, whimbrel and dotterel were on his list. There was abundance, too, of birds of prey, eagles, peregrines and goshawks, but these were already proscribed: " half a crown is given for an eagle, a shilling for a hawk or a hooded crow." Other menaces to game as well as to the livestock of the farm were foxes, " in these parts very ravenous, feeding on roes, sheep and even the goats."

He found the human males of Upper Deeside lazy, except when hunting animals or pursuing amusement. The women he deemed industrious but " most remarkably plain." The housing he deemed " shocking to humanity" and their way of living " poor and nasty." Not for Mr. Pennant, passing Balmoral on his way to what he called Bolliter (Ballater to-day), the Stevensonian glimpse of the Highland country places where the young fair maidens have quiet eyes. In his narrative he repeated his disgust with the looks of the locals, thinking nothing could be worse until he met the fish-wives of Aberdeen where " the *ne plus ultra* of hard features " was on view.

Tastes in human features, as in landscape, vary, and a man who described the sparkling falls and peaty pools of

the Tilt in its glorious race under the majesty of Ben-y-Ghlo
as " dreary " was obviously queer of sight and not to be
trusted in matters of aesthetics. Fortunately, one visitor who
followed a stag-party up to Forest Lodge had a more
sympathetic eye and a better faculty of appraisal. For her
the view here was beyond description and the bliss incom-
parable too. That spellbound spectator was, of course,
Queen Victoria, who drove up the Glen from Blair Atholl
where she was staying as the Duke's guest in September,
1844. To Prince Albert the scene was equally a cause for
ecstasy; and there was also abundant exercise for the Prince
as rifleman. But the technique of shooting was now
radically altered from the old massacre once practised by the
chieftains and relished by their guests.

One of the great features of the ancient Stag Parties was
the feasting. Taylor paid ample tribute to the catering
among the Lonchards in Mar. Pennant, recalling the great
hunt made by the Earl of Atholl for the amusement of
James V, quotes a description by Sir David Lindsay of the
Mount, author of that much revived and much esteemed
Morality Play *The Three Estaits*. A palace of green timber
and bricks was specially set up near Blair and the floors
covered deep in flowers. The walls were hung with fine
tapestry and arrases of silk, and there were glass windows on
every side. " This palace was as pleasantly decored, with
all the necessaries pertaining to a prince, as it had been his
own palace-royal at home." Lindsay said little of the
gigantic scale of the hunting, for which " Thousands of
vassals surrounded a great tract of country," but he was
explicit about the feasting.

The liquors included " wine, both white and claret,
Malvery, Muscadel, Hippocras, Aquavitae." All con-

ceivable species of meat and game were prepared by "proper stewards, cunning baxters, excellent cooks and potingars with confections and drugs for their deserts," while specially constructed pools were stocked with salmon, trout and " all other kind of delicate fishes that could be gotten in fresh waters." The King stayed three days and nights in this mixed orgy of carnage and collation. The Earl of Atholl was said to be paying a thousand pounds a day to provide it; in the currency values of these days such an outlay was prodigious. Foolish, no doubt, but interesting evidence that even in the remote Highlands in the Middle Ages there was no lack of amenity and of luxury for a nobleman who chose to command these things, no lack of wealth to pay for them, and no lack of willing labour to provide them. The gentry did not propose to go killing on an empty stomach.

CHAPTER SIX

New Methods

THE organisation of Deeside sport when Queen Victoria and Prince Albert took over Balmoral was on a much simpler scale than in the years of the great assemblies of the Lairds and the Tinchels. It was no longer necessary to mass the prey for dispatch by bow and blunderbuss. It was Albert's own Germany that had so greatly improved the early firearms that the Elector John George II of Saxony who reigned from 1656 to 1680 is said, during his life, to have killed 62,575 deer, 22,298 wild boars, 239 bears and 2,196 wolves. That was something to make even an Earl of Mar look up and wonder, and to evoke even more enraptured and excruciating sonnets from a London Water Poet.

In a book on *The Sporting Rifle* by " The Ruffle " (1951) the invention of breech-loading is also attributed to Germany; the Central European Jaegers were famous for their weapons as well as for their skill. The author explains that when deerstalking became a popular sport and replaced deer-driving in the Highlands during the nineteenth century there were the advances of the conical-shaped bullet: the calibre was larger than it is to-day. Prince Albert probably used a half-inch lead bullet with a small charge of black powder in his muzzle-loader and that weapon would be sighted for 200 yards. The modern stalker, with a lower calibre breech-loader, smokeless powder, and a soft-headed bullet, has much more chance of killing outright.

Critics of " Balmorality " should be relieved to learn that the shooting there, during the life of the Prince Consort, was of a simple and austere type. Albert had experienced the relics of the old *battue en masse* during his first visit to Scotland and during that stay at Taymouth Castle with the Marquis of Breadalbane which did so much to put both Prince and Queen in love with Scottish country. True, there was not quite the massing of man-power known to the Earl of Mar, but with " Breadalbane himself beating and three hundred Highlanders out," it was certainly an occasion. The bag, " nineteen roedeer, several hares and pheasants and three brace of grouse " must surely have been understated by the Queen. (Possibly Breadalbane's men, like the Tinchels described by Taylor, knew how " to lick their fingers.") Albert, however, was delighted with his " excellent sport."

But the sporting life was not for Albert to be a routine of easy sessions before driven game in the manner of the old " unmatchable huntings " in the Braes of Mar. Next day, he was one of a party " walking up " grouse in heavy rain from nine till three, " wading up to his knees in bogs." Nine brace were bagged, a modest achievement. On another day he was up at five in the morning to go deer-stalking. He returned at three, sunburned and exhausted, but with a stag to his credit. He wrote in a letter that " this curious sport," as the Queen phrased it, was " one of the most fatiguing, as it is one of the most interesting of pursuits."

The constant crawling had been hard work for a man so

zealous at the desk in most months of the year, and his young companion, Campbell of Menzie, had been "extremely active," setting a stern example of agility with the advantage of better training. During his stay at Blair Atholl two years later the Prince also had some hard going on the mountains above Glen Tilt. But that noble forest of Atholl did not yield him lucky days. Once, wrote the Queen, " my poor Albert had not fired a shot for fear of spoiling the whole thing, but had been running about a good deal." On another occasion, " his rifle would not go off when he could have shot some fine harts." But he came back " merry and cheerful." There was something in that Highland air.

Shooting at Balmoral, when that castle had been taken over, was largely a matter of a walk with a gun or rifle and a couple of ghillies. It could thus be usefully combined with the Queen's passion for mountain climbs. During the first ascent of Lochnagar (September, 1848) Albert shot a brace of ptarmigan *en route*. Later in that month there was a " royal " killed in the forest of Ballochbuie as the result of a drive, but this was a small manœuvre and no major operation with scores of beaters. And so it continued. There would be a carriage outing; if deer were seen, Albert would jump out and fire. The Queen might use her pencil and paper to celebrate the deed, if he had been lucky and the prey was worthy of it. She had something of Landseer's taste for an imposing carcass. There was the autumn day in 1852 when the cairn was raised on Craig Gowan to celebrate " our taking possession of this dear place." In the afternoon Albert decided to seize a last chance in the woods, for there was to be the dismal return to London immediately after. He shot a stag, " a magnificent animal." Victoria sat down to sketch it on a scrap of paper produced by a ghillie—and quite a good sketch it is. Her first-born, " poor Vicky," on this occasion also sat down—on a wasps' nest. She was much stung before being rescued by another of the devoted Highlanders. Royal the party might be, but it was all very like any family picnic with the ants swarming and the wasps about. The shooting at this time was usually not more than a part of a domestic outing.

The capture of salmon, a sport natural to the Dee so famous for its " run " of this fish, was not then a skilled pursuit of the fly-fisher. It was conducted, instead, upon a larder-basis. The weapon principally in use was the leister or spear; even in Queen Victoria's time the Balmoral salmon were thus spiked or driven into nets. There is no mention of the Prince Consort as a devotee of fly-fishing. In September 1850 he joined Victoria and their guests at the riverside above the bridge where " all our tenants are assembled with poles and spears, or rather ' leisters ' for catching salmon." These tenants, to the number of a hundred—" a very pretty effect "—waded about; they prodded and poked under the stones where the fish might be lying in order to stab them or stir them into the nets held ready. There was much excitement but no success at first; even after moving upstream, there was no better luck; indeed, there was almost a calamity. This exercise had its risks.

Two men, one of whom could not swim, entered a deep pool and the non-swimmer had to be rescued with a gallant plunge by Dr. Robertson, the manager of the Balmoral estates, an "amiable" man and much approved by the Prince Consort and the Queen. Later on in the day seven fish were either netted or speared. " Though Albert stood in the water some time he caught nothing," is his wife's succinct report. Fortunately, the sun was hot and the scene was picturesque; it was pleasant to bask on the banks and the Queen felt the need of Landseer's pencil. The Dee is what is called an early river, and has its great run of salmon in the spring; so the autumn visitations of royalty were unlikely to be met with the best of Aberdeenshire fishing. When visits have been made in May, Balmoral has offered the caster of a fly a more delicate exercise than was endured by the Prince Consort as he paddled, leister in hand, on that sunny September day in 1850.

In the matter of refreshment there was none of the old guzzling and swilling at Balmoral; if there had been, the critics of the Monarchy would have had plenty to say about it, and *Punch* would doubtless have pelleted the shooters with the radical rancour which was then its political temper. The Castle by the Dee was to be a home, not a palace; its tables would carry a good sufficiency of native food, but simplicity should be the rule; and so it remains.

In the Victorian period the quantity of eating and drinking was beginning to decline after the excesses of the Regency. But some notions of what could be absorbed, especially by followers of the hounds, were still high, as readers of Surtees know. The advice given by Scrope on the drink-ration proper to Stag Parties is interesting, since he wrote (about life on the far side of Glen Tilt) during the early visits of Victoria and Albert to Scotland. He was advocating temperance for the sportsman; too much of canakin's clink would mean unsteady hands the next day. " Wine and poetry go joyously together; Bacchus and Apollo were aye boon companions. But I never heard of Diana having attached herself to the jolly god." (Scrope obviously had a classical education.) However, having delivered severe warnings against the union of stalking with " pottle-deep potations," he concedes this much to the stalker's thirst; " The best part of a bottle of champagne may be allowed at dinner; this is not only venial but salutary. A few tumblers of brandy and soda-water are greatly to be commended, for they are cooling. Whisky cannot reasonably be objected to, for it is an absolute necessary, and does not come under the head of intemperance, but rather, as Dogberry says, or ought to say, ' it comes by nature.' Gingerbeer I hold to be a dropsical, insufficient, and unmanly beverage. I pray you avoid it."

The ration seems sufficient, even for a " drouthy " man. All whisky-drinkers will be grateful for the observations about their favourite and its absolution from guilt. Scrope seems to have regarded it as the native water of the land and so not in the category of alcoholic liquors. Queen Victoria's John Brown would have approved the notion that whisky " comes by nature." It is remarkable that ginger-beer should be mentioned at all, if only to be properly dismissed for its effeminacy, insufficiency, and dropsicality.

In the early nineteenth century the sources of the Dee and the Cairngorms provided such sport that fashionable visitors were taking houses some time before the Royal selection of Braemar. The Duke of Leeds was at Old Mar Lodge in the eighteen-forties and in 1847 he entertained the Grand Duke of Nassau together with three German Barons. Lady Catherine Carnegie, who attended the Gathering at Braemar Castle that year, recorded in her diary that Braemar was full for the occasion; but there was much less accommodation then than there is now. She had to make the long and hard drive over the Cairnwell to the Spital of Glenshee to get a bed. She also records that " the Duke looked very plebeian and unaristocratic in his Highland costume." The Gathering was, of course, quite a small, parochial affair and the racing and caber-tossing were as commendably brief as the subsequent hospitality of the Farquharsons was commendably cordial. It is interesting that she called caber-tossing by the title of " turning the bar."

There was no reluctance on the part of ladies to join the Stag Parties and to take an active hand with a rifle, though there may have been some male hesitation about these intrusions. Lady Catherine called at Aboyne to dine (mid-day) on her way to Braemar; she reported " an excellent dinner of salmon, chicken, mutton chops, cold grouse and porter." What did our ancestors mean when they wrote like that of their meals? Did Lady Catherine just copy down the hotel menu or did she really absorb a helping of each? The porter, by the way, is surprising; it sounds as " plebeian and unaristocratic " as the kilted Duke of Leeds had looked. Lady Catherine then called on Lady Aboyne at her castle, but the latter was not to be found; she had gone out stalking with her husband. The party at Old Mar Lodge also contained some markswomen of whom Mrs. Horatio Ross won renown as the most skilled. The Duchess of Bedford was another devotee of hard days on the hills.

In view of the amount of clothing that a lady would then have to carry on a climb and a crawl, the moorland achievements of these early Victorians are the more remarkable. Queen Victoria herself did not shoot, or at least never put on record any experiments with gun or rifle. But she climbed on foot, as well as on pony, continually and in the roughest places. She certainly was not attired with the simplicity, aiming at ease of movement, favoured by the girls who nowadays emerge from Youth Hostels to do a day of peak-bagging; when a male mountaineer found one of these sparsely-clad heroines gasping and " peching," as the Scots say, in the midst of a stiff ascent, he aptly remarked, " You climb in short pants."

The gentleman's sporting outfit is now, at least on expert recommendation, and under pressure of high-powered salesmanship, a complete and costly change from town wear. It has to be a strong shield against wind and weather. " A green and brown daubed overblouse of weather-proof material, breeches of stout cord, gaiters and boots " are one prescription for defiance of the climate. Mackintosh zippers and stormproof jackets in all varieties are to be considered. Were our forefathers so much tougher than we are—or merely careless? For the pictures of the deer-stalker of the 1840s show him in a frock-coat and long check trousers of a tight cut. Stiff collars and a flowing bow tie clothe the neck in some cases. Sometimes spats were worn over the boots, sometimes not. The genteel combatant of the Monarch of the Glen could have walked out of a Dickens illustration and into the Piccadilly of his day without anybody thinking him oddly garbed.

The pictures in Scrope's volume, already mentioned, are " engravings and woodcuts from designs by Edwin and Charles Landseer and the author." So they afford authentic evidence of what was worn at the time of writing: the ghillies go kilted, while the distinguished visitors are always in the coat and pantaloons of at least informal town wear. In an engraving by Hunt from a painting by E. C. Turner called " Grouse Shooting by the Southerner " the gentlemen counting their " bag " (one brace visible) are wearing top-hats and seem perfectly equipped for any West End occasion. There are no signs of wrapping up. But the pictures never admit the existence of rain. On many days there must have been some overcoats taken; but it is worth noting that Queen Victoria, in her *Journals*, though candid about dampness and even drenchings, says very little of the counter-measures, apart from an occasional allusion to a plaid or rug in the carriage. The Sporting Prints of Highland life in the forties proclaim eternal sunshine; but that must have been an artist's convention. The Leaves from the *Journals* tell a different story.

King Edward VII had learned shooting as a boy. At the age of seventeen he wrote to his tutor about his killing two " royals," one of 17 stone 2 pounds and another of 16 stone 3 pounds, whereas his father had only dispatched one. After his marriage he stayed every year at Abergeldie Castle, which became the usual Deeside residence of the Prince of Wales, and there made holiday with shooting by day and with cards at night. In 1871 he asked Mr. Gladstone, who was then the Minister in Residence at Balmoral, to drive over and dine. Gladstone was charmed by his manners, but not so happy about his morals, at least in the small matter of gaming. Did not the Prince play cards for money? " After dinner he invited me to play whist," the Prime Minister recorded. " I said, ' For love, sir?' He said, ' Well, shillings and half a crown on the rubber,' to which I submitted." For the Prince to mention such paltry stakes was a nice point of manners.

This entry in Gladstone's diary does not relate who won and how much. Twenty years later the Prince was to be involved in the wretched Tranby Croft case when one of the party was charged with cheating. There followed the well-known action for slander, which caused such embarrassment to the Royal Family since it reflected, though unfairly, on the company kept by the Prince. We need not suppose that when the Liberal leader played cards for money at Abergeldie, he gave any just cause for Labouchère's later and much-adopted remark that Mr. G. always had the ace of trumps up his sleeve and then explained that God had put it there.

When he succeeded to the throne and to Balmoral, King Edward VII loved to entertain large shooting parties, but by that time he was close upon sixty years of age and growing stout. He naturally preferred for himself the less strenuous grouse-drives and the covert shooting of driven pheasants at Sandringham or at the great country houses in England or in Europe where he was often an autumn or a winter guest. He could, like his son, King George V, take his place worthily among the great shots of the day in a kind of sport which was once a matter of *battues* and of record bags, but has now dwindled away.

The reason for that change is obviously to some extent economic: such shoots meant careful and expensive rearing of pheasants and also their expensive protection by well-trained keepers from the raids of vermin and of poachers. After the first great war, and still more after the second, not only the keepers, but also the beaters and loaders essential to a *battue* became scarce or unobtainable. Cartridges, too, which used to be a penny each soared to fivepence. In one day at Hall Barn, Beaconsfield, George V is said to have fired 1760 cartridges from his guns in a single day.[1] The present cost of that ammunition would be well over thirty pounds quite apart from wage-bills and tips. Other costs mounted severely. The incomes of the country gentry were no less severely cut. So the winter shooting of carefully

[1] *King George V*, by John Gore, p. 230.

fostered birds, with " bags " running into the hundreds and thousands, disappeared and few can regret its going. Some of the practitioners had never much liked it. John Gore records that George V, though a most able shot with a perfect style and precision of marksmanship and therefore one of the few most expert performers among the well-stocked coverts at Sandringham, preferred to go out as " a marauder " on the Norfolk marshes accompanied only by one or two of his farmer friends.

This was a far more strenuous exercise and involved the use of manœuvre to get near the target and not only sureness of hand and eye. He could excel in those mammoth drives such as that at Hall Barn on 18th December, 1913, when he was one of seven guns who accounted for 3,937 pheasants on a day, but he had a great relish for flushing a few wood-cock when he tramped the woods as one of a small company or practised the fowler's art among the meres and marshes near his Norfolk home. The Sandringham estate was the creation of his father and the particular joy of himself; he was long housed at York Cottage, of which Sir Harold Nicolson has given so vividly sombre a picture in his life of George V. Gloomy or not, it provided the bright days of the King's winter. But he was happy, too, at Balmoral. Both of these he preferred to Windsor.

Testimony to the skill of his shooting has been made by one of his beaters (or would-be beaters) who was soon to become one of his subjects' best writers in many branches of letters. In that late summer of 1921 Eric Linklater, with two fellow-students of Aberdeen University, " in the same plight of poverty " as himself, took a thrifty vacation by camping in Upper Deeside or, to be more exact, in one of the glens leading from Dee to Don. They were hired by a nearby owner or renter of a moor as beaters for four weeks; they earned 8s. a day for five days in each week. This meant walking as much as twenty or twenty-five mountainous miles a day, often through deep heather. There were certain other compensations, not fully covenanted, in the way of fish and fowl for the stewpot which hung over the fire in the evening beside their bell tent. " The grouse,"[1] Linklater has written, " is an excellent bird, but created for sport and table and so no one had compunction in guiding it towards its appointed death." On this convenient interpretation of Nature's purposes in the matter of avian evolution many people have agreed.

When their employers gave the student-beaters a holiday the young men decided that they would, if they could, beat for the King. He was to be shooting nearby. At Balmoral the deer-forest is to the south of the river on the slopes of Lochnagar and round Loch Muick, while the grouse moors are to the north of Dee. On this occasion the guns were to be on the hill called Geallaig which rises to a height of 2,439 feet, just opposite Abergeldie Castle. The volunteer beaters applied to the head keeper when the shooting party arrived, but the labour supply was already sufficient. They stood about waiting for the off-chance of a job and were noticed. The King and the Duke of York both came up and talked to them.

" The King, in his voice that was rough about the edges and genial in essence, asked who we were and what we did. Shyly, in overlapping words, we told him, and with a flicker of amusement in his beard—looking at our posture—he asked, ' Have you been in the Army?' We told him the names of our regiments and he talked to us a little longer;

<hr>

[1] *A Year of Space* by Eric Linklater.

and at his right shoulder the Duke of York looked at us all the while with steady and percipient eyes. He was of our generation, he knew us better than the King. The old King was quite simply the Chief of the Clan, the Captain of the Ship; but the Duke had trodden the years that we had trodden, and he did not smile when the King smiled."

The King then apologised for his inability to be an employer, as the team of beaters had already been made up and had gone off to start the drive. But he could, and did, invite them to stay and watch. So, delighted with this courtesy, they were hidden in a hollow behind the King's butt and waited for the grouse.

" They came in great numbers and at prodigious speed, for the wind was with them and the slope of the hill determined their course, and from the edge of the coveys the King took them down with inerrable aim. We knew, by that time, something about good shooting, and every bird that fell to the King's gun was dead in the air before it dropped. When a large covey came, and another closely followed, there were two, three, four dead birds in the air before the first had fallen. It was shooting as the ordinary first-class shot may dream of shooting. It was the very summit of marksmanship, the nonpareil of shooting, and while we watched—and we knew what to look for—not a bird came fluttering down, but every one was a meteor falling or a plummet dropping straight. Two or three of our own guns, across the valley, were good; but the King who had treated us so gently was supernacular."

Those in doubt about the last word and think it must be a misprint for supernatural can consult the dictionary with confidence. The supernacular is a liquor to be drunk to the last drop, a wine of the highest quality, anything excellent of its kind. Had Queen Victoria known of this classicism, she might have used it frequently to convey the raptures and the ecstasies of a day round the Balmoral moors or the Cairngorm summits; but it might have been less applicable to the marksmanship of her husband than to that of George V.

And of George VI too. The sporting life of the Highlands was not a major interest of Edward VIII, but his younger brother was in his earlier years tireless as well as proficient. When his leg trouble made the sport more difficult the modern advantage of cross-country motoring in cars of particular toughness came to his aid; the rows of grouse-butts that once needed a laborious approach are now more easily attained. The Duke of Edinburgh has inherited an embarrassing tradition of skill upon the grouse-moors; it is said that he has now thoroughly mastered the craft.

The opponents of blood-sports can fairly argue that it is an occupation unworthy of civilised man to rear and hand-feed birds in order to turn them loose and then shoot them for fun. But the Highlands sports are not of this kind. The grouse is the natural bird of the hills and would multiply to such an extent that it would go hungry and contract disease from overcrowding if it were not kept down by its enemies. Nature's opponents are the birds of prey and the vermin. Before shooting began the moors round Balmoral must have had their coveys of grouse rigorously thinned by the raids of fox, hawk and eagle. But, by the time of Pennant's visit (1769), man was jealous of those poachers on preserves that he assumed, with the power of the shotgun on this side, to be his. So there was a price on every raptorial head, with half a crown for an eagle and a shilling for a hooded crow. Later on, with their natural enemies extirpated, the grouse, less harried by the talons, were confronted, increasingly, with the guns. If they had had no enemies at all, they would have been confronted with nature's own remedy for excessive populations, which is not a kindly one.

In the case of deer-stalking there is an urgent need of thinning the herds. Nature, by sending exceptionally severe winters, can supply its own cure for overbreeding and that is certainly not a gentle therapy. If the winters remain open and the feeding in the glens is sufficient the numbers will rise and there will be consequent and damaging invasion of farms and even gardens when the next winter brings the deer down from the high corries. So man has to defend his own food supply. To provide and maintain high fences everywhere is not only an extremely laborious and expensive operation; it also means that the deer, successfully penned back in the hills in excessive numbers, will soon be thinned by the slow death of starvation. That the herds should be limited by the rifle-bullet is a merciful solution, provided that the shooting is efficient and that a wounded beast is immediately followed up and destroyed as swiftly as possible; to do so is always the rule on a well-run estate. It is the raiding party of poachers from the towns, seeking saleable venison, that may inflict wanton damage and pain by reckless shooting and wounding. It is the commercial killer, not the sportsman, who is chargeable with cruelty.

The stalking of deer involves so much exertion, as Prince Albert immediately discovered, as well as skill in manœuvre and in the tactics of getting close enough to shoot with some certainty of a clean kill, that the man or woman who has dispatched a stag has been engaged in a battle of endurance and intelligence. There is no comparison between this kind of shooting and that of the driven pheasant, except in the demand on the eye and the ready hand. A stalker is at odds with Nature as well as with his prey. Eric Linklater, in the same chapter that contained his portrait of George V at the butts on Geallaig, has recounted that he has only once shot a red deer and that did not occur until he was fifty, too late to form a habit. " The excitement was deeper as the labour to attain it was more strenuous." He had had a whole day of clambering and of frustration by shots denied on a great, treeless forest; then came a final climb and crawl until his heart seemed " swollen to the size of a Rugby football." Then there fell upon him the sharp fear that all was lost once again. Fortunately the stag rose and " stood superb, his great head high and turned a little towards me, his off foreleg crooked at the knee for action. I put up my rifle and fired."

There the stag lay. " He was dead, and I loved him dearly. For a moment, I suppose, I loved myself, and him I loved because he contributed to me. But whatever the niceties and shadows of the sensation, it was both a profound and exalted feeling—profound because its origin lay in the heart of an ancestral Pict, perhaps, and exalted because I had driven my body to an exertion far beyond its custom and killed my stag—my only stag—with the cleanness of instant death. And we stood two thousand feet above the sea, with the bare, enormous forest all about us, and the wide, unsullied sky above. . . ."

The humanitarian may still shudder at this Landseerian picture. But this pride in victory is a multiple joy. There had been hard-won triumph over wind and weather, moor and peat, and as well over the scenting powers and inborn cunning of the stag. The smallest of God's creatures as well

as the large heights and heathery distances are the enemy of
the stalker: Linklater had to make his shot with his chin
on the peat and his neck tormented by a fly. The Highland
' cleg ' or horse-fly is the very devil of a combatant, attacking
unseen. Queen Victoria's beloved Loch Muick was famous
for its midges and a host of Highland midges in search of
its supper is an army with daggers. There must, one fancies,
have been many a guest at Balmoral who went blithely to
the forest in the morning and came home less likely to sing
in his bath

> "*My heart's in the Highlands, my heart is not here,*
> *My heart's in the Highlands, a-chasing the deer.*"

It was all very well for John Taylor three and a half centuries
ago when the "unmatchable hunting" was a session in the
glen with herds driven before the bow and the harquebus.
But had the then Earl of Mar and his numerous fellow-
chieftains been under the compulsion of crawling on their
bellies in the corries of the Cairngorms they might not have
gathered with such zest to show their prowess in carnage and
in filling of the larder.

Conviviality continued to be a feature of Balmoral's
sporting life. Queen Victoria did not contradict the opinion
of Mr. Scrope, already quoted, that " whisky comes by
nature." She liked to see the ghillies merry and did not
blench when they were " fou." After the shooting there
would be the somewhat savage rite of inspecting the dead
bodies of the stags by torchlight. Then came dancing, " all
of which " wrote Sir Frederick Ponsonby,[1] " was very
pretty, but after she left it became an orgy," a fact of which
she can hardly have been ignorant. Sir Frederick also states

---

[1] *Recollections of Three Reigns* by Sir Frederick Ponsonby, p. 151.

that the amount of whisky consumed by the servants was truly stupendous; whenever any guest went out stalking the ghillie drew a whisky ration of a whole bottle, as well as swallowing a good tot before he started. It was unlikely that the guest would drink his full share of so large an allowance and so the ghillie in full employment had " whisky galore."

Another generous rule in Queen Victoria's time ordained that, when she was driving out, a bottle of whisky should be put under the coachman's seat in case of accidents. It was viewed, philanthropically, as part of the Red Cross outfit. She had seen a collapsed figure by the roadside thus revived and she had memories of her own disaster when the carriage overturned on the way back from Glen Muick, and there was only claret for comfort. There was obviously room here for a little misapplication of the therapeutic bottle!

It is curious that Queen Victoria, who is regarded to-day as very strict in all matters of conduct, and certainly was strict with those close to her, was extremely tolerant in her attitude to drinking—at least among her Highlanders. How ready she was to condone at the mere sight of a kilt and at the sound of a Scottish voice! Of these Scots it could almost be said that in her eyes they could do no wrong. Even so solemn an occasion as the anniversary of the Prince Consort's birthday was honoured, after the rites had been duly observed, with liberal libations among all the workers on the estate, which Ponsonby said left many of the celebrants prostrate. By that time the Queen was not there and she was not returning to look for abuse of her hospitality.

It was actually King Edward VII who imposed a discipline on these habits. Some of the stalkers can hardly have liked his reforms when he substituted a flask for a bottle as the day's ration for the hill and even dismissed a man of thirty years' service for being drunk when the luncheon interval arrived; it was thought that the offender might lose his pension altogether; in the end he retained it so long as he kept away. It is one of the little ironies of history that the son, famous for gaiety, of a supposedly strict mother should have stepped in to put a limit to the uses (or abuses) of " the social glass," or, to be more accurate, " the social bottle."

CHAPTER SEVEN

John Brown

JOHN BROWN, who was to be such an abiding comfort to Queen Victoria and the Prince Consort, such an enigma and at times such an annoyance to her family and visitors, such a source of raw material for gossip, and such a treasure to the mid-Victorian Schools for Scandal, was the son of a Deeside farmer. James Brown, his father, rented from the Farquharsons the holding known as Bridgend of Bush lying to the north-west of Crathie village. Among the forests and the deer-forests some usable acres lay along the road which runs up from Balmoral to Glen Gairn; but no farmer's life in these high places was ever easy. The air is brisk and, despite hard work and exposure, longevity may thrive on it. James Brown had married Margaret Leys, the daughter of a blacksmith at Aberarder, and both John's parents achieved a grand old age, his father dying at eighty-six and his mother at eighty-seven.

There were nine sons, three of whom emigrated. It was rare for the whole of large families to survive in those days and the Browns lost three boys at the ages of three, ten and seventeen and a daughter at fourteen. Their famous son, John, later on to be entitled John Brown, Esquire, by Her

Majesty and given a house within the royal precincts of the Castle, had a life of moderate length. He did not survive a severe chill caught by driving in an open trap on a bleak day, and died at Windsor in March, 1883, aged only fifty-six. One feels that he should have lasted longer. He had been a pillar of Highland manhood in his Deeside youth and most active as a ghillie in the great hills; in those early years an open trap, even on a bleak day, in the Home Counties of England would have been like first-class travel to him. But he had softened as an indoor servant and his consumption of whisky, a drink easily and safely absorbed amid Highland air and exercise, had not diminished when he became the "Johannes Factotum" of the Queen, living an indoor life in castle and palace, a stationary, if not sedentary, existence.

He was not an ignorant boy. We know from the life of Robert Burns and his training under the tutor Murdoch how intense, though narrow in range, could be the book-learning on a Scottish farm. In *Queen Victoria's John Brown* by E. E. P. Tisdall, it is stated that Jamie Brown, the father, had been to a University and had spent some years as a schoolmaster before he had enough money to rent a farm. He even wrote a guide to the neighbourhood. The occasional affectation of Burns that he was an unlettered ploughboy would hardly have been followed by any of the Crathie Browns, who were more likely to be proud of their accomplishments. A far nook of wildest Caledonia might be their home, but even there education was well established. There had been a school at Crathie since 1710 and there were several local Charity Schools sustained by the Society for the Propagation of Christian Knowledge; Catholic schooling was also provided at Braemar. Ruled by a parent who had himself been at the dominie's desk, Bridgend of Bush was likely to be a literate house.

As an Aberdeenshire Brown myself, with ancestral roots in Donside, I have a natural interest in the origins of our now widespread tribe. One theory is that the Browns, and the Blacks too, became numerous during and after the general persecution which followed the collapse in 1746 of the Stuart rising. There was little hope and much danger for members of those clans which had taken part in it. It was forbidden to wear the accoutrements of a Highlander and to carry the usual arms. It was dangerous to own the name of one of the families or to be a sept of the families most associated with " the '45." Therefore, a prudent man might prefer, after hiding, to reappear with a name undistinguished and so unlikely to arouse suspicion. Hence, it is surmised, there was during the second half of the eighteenth century a diminishing of the " Macs " and an irruption of Browns and Blacks.

I do not know to what extent this is true, but it is a significant fact that the Browns and Blacks scarcely appear at all in the population rolls of Upper Deeside at the end of the seventeenth century. The Rev. John Stirton, in his *History of the United Parishes of Crathie and Braemar*, includes " ane list of poleable persons within the Parishes of Kindrochit and Crathie in 1696," that is, nineteen years before the standard of the Old Pretender was raised in this very district in the first attempt to re-establish the Stuart dynasty. Many of the names most familiar in Aberdeenshire are on the list; Shaw, Simpson, Bain, Brebner, Mair, Mitchell and Keir are there in plenty in addition to numerous Farquharsons, some Grants and Gordons, and a variety of names beginning with " Mac." Since the population of the Highlands was then very much larger than it is now, the " poleables " of these parishes make up a very long list from which the Blacks are wholly absent and the Browns limited to one mention. Since they were later to become numerous, this can be taken to suggest the arrival of those names during the ensuing century.

It is worth noting that, while so many of the Upper Deeside names were not Gaelic in 1696, Gaelic was the general language in use in that district until the beginning of the nineteenth century; but most of the people were bilingual by then. Consequently, if they had business to transact, they could do so in English—or, to be more exact, in the form of Scots in use in this region. The rolls that Stirton printed contain, incidentally, some names which may be of interest to collectors of such curios. There is, for example, the family of Ego and also that of Ladikins. Students of John Brown's later career might consider him a natural cousin of the Deeside Egos.

Mr. Tisdall mentions a claim of the Crathie Browns to have been descended from an aristocratic and obstinate Covenanter, Sir John Brown of Fordels, in Fifeshire, who died, for his convictions, while a prisoner in Leith. One of his sons, it is said, escaped from Scotland to the Low Countries; he returned in safer times and became a Professor of Divinity at Aberdeen. He bred a large family and Scottish families are accustomed to a wide dispersion for economic and professional reasons. So the Browns of Bridgend of Bush may have descended from one who moved west from Aberdeen instead of being native Highlanders who had found security in a new and inconspicuous name. If the immigrant Browns had been children of Fife arriving by way of Aberdeen, they would probably have had to learn their Gaelic instead of absorbing it with the milk and porridge.

The John Brown, who was to become such a Palace potentate, worked, when he was a boy of sixteen, on the farm of Crathienaird, which was close to his father's place. He moved a little way from there, crossing the River Dee to be engaged as a helping lad in the stables of the old house of Balmoral. His new employer, the tenant of Balmoral, was Sir Robert Gordon. That was in 1842. Fortunately for himself, Brown stayed in that establishment; so when Queen Victoria first leased the old Balmoral in 1848, John became a junior ghillie; he was well trained to take sportsmen on the hills or fishermen on the river and ready to interpret, should any of the visitors be eager to understand the Gaelic conversation of the district. He was, therefore, " on the strength " when the all-important change of tenancy was made. It was to prove a lucky day that had taken him to seek work with Sir Robert.

He is first referred to by the Queen in her *Journal* entry of September 11, 1849. After she had heard the children repeat some poetry in German, a drive-and-ride excursion was made, at first with carriage and then on pony, round and above Loch Muick. The ghillies mentioned on that occasion were Grant, Macdonald, Jemmie and Charles Coutts, John Brown and old John Gordon. This time Macdonald gained the favourable mention. He led the Queen's pony and was " extremely useful and attentive." Brown was watching and learning. He attracted notice in the following year. The Queen, describing a row on Loch Muick on the evening of September 16, with one of the Couttses piping, mentions " J. Brown " as one of the oarsmen. The day's entry in the *Journal* carries this undated note:

" The same who, in 1858, became my regular attendant out of doors everywhere in the Highlands; who commenced as ghillie in 1849, and was selected by Albert and me to go with my carriage. In 1851 he entered our service permanently, and began in that year leading my pony, and advanced step by step by his good conduct and intelligence. His attention, care, and faithfulness cannot be exceeded; and the state of my health, which of late years has been sorely tried and weakened, renders such qualifications most valuable, and indeed, most needful in a constant attendant upon all occasions. He has since (in December, 1865), most deservedly, been promoted to be an upper servant, and my permanent personal attendant. He has all the independence and elevated feelings peculiar to the Highland race, and is singularly straightforward, simple-minded, kind-hearted, and disinterested; always ready to oblige; and of a discretion rarely to be met with. He is now in his fortieth year. His father was a small farmer, who lived at the Bush on the opposite side of Balmoral. He is the second of nine brothers—three of whom have died —two are in Australia and New Zealand, two are living in the neighbourhood of Balmoral; and the youngest, Archie (Archiebald) is valet to our own Leopold, and is an excellent, trustworthy young man."

Henceforward John Brown's attendance was regular and his prowess as a guide and pony-man was regularly noted. He gave particular pleasure on September 30, 1859, during an excursion to Inchrory; this lies to the north of Balmoral between Ben Avon and the hill known as The Brown Cow. Grant and Brown travelled on foot at five miles an hour.

Brown displayed " that vigorous, light, elastic tread which is quite astonishing." Grant, although a senior ghillie, was keeping up the same pace; but he received no similar tribute. Finally, the nimble Brown led the Queen's pony up the Glaschoil Hill " at an amazing pace." He had confirmed previous impressions of his outstanding usefulness and energy. The day's entry ends with the familiar adjective " enchanted " and expresses the usual craving for more and more of this Highland magic. " How I wish we could travel about in this way and see all the wild spots in the Highlands."

Brown assisted in the ascent of Ben MacDhui a week later; during this climb the Queen had to walk some of the way to the summit of 4,297 feet while " Albert and Bertie walked the whole time." It is conceivable that the Prince of Wales, lacking a stride as light and elastic as John Brown's, may have taken a dislike to Ben MacDhui. He certainly took one to John Brown, if not then, at least during later years. In that case Bertie would have had a sympathetic friend in a groom called Batterbury who had " seemed anything but happy " when " with thin boots and gaiters " he followed the Queen and Prince Consort to the summit of Lochnagar. " He hardly ever attended me after this," remarks the *Journal* tersely.

The summit of Ben MacDhui was shrouded in mist for some time and the wind bitter. It was on this occasion that Brown remarked of the Prince, " Everyone on the estate says there never was so kind a master; I am sure that our only wish is to give satisfaction." He further expressed his happiness in walking with people always so contented. He did not achieve his first advancement in the household by the gruffness and brusqueness which he was later to display in higher office.

In 1860 the ghillie was becoming the indoor servant. The man who had excelled in the stalking and gralloching (gutting) of stags had to learn parlour tricks. During the first of the Great Expeditions, when the royal couple with Lady Churchill and General Grey were driving and riding abroad with the pretence of being only Lord and Lady Churchill and Party, Brown showed himself the imperfect actor by suddenly using the term " Your Majesty "; in any case, the " incognito " did not prove effective and the cavalcade was saluted in Granton. After a stay at an inn, both Brown and Grant were told that they should have done the waiting at dinner and breakfast, since the ears of strange servants were not welcome in the room. The Queen knew that Brown with three other men and two maids had been " very merry " in the Commercial Room. It is understandable that, after a long day's travel with much walking over rough ground at the head of a pony, the ghillies had no eagerness to be enrolled as waiters. It was much more pleasant to sit with one's feet up and a bottle handy amid the mirth of the Commercial Room.

But the absence and the merriment were forgiven and almost at once Brown was described as perfect, " handy and willing to do everything and anything and to overcome every difficulty, which makes him one of my best servants anywhere." He soon showed at least a moderate mastery of the art of waiting, while continuing to be the peerless escort on the roads and mountains. He knew all the royal whims and had an eye to provide their satisfaction. The Queen was fond of white heather; Brown was always the first to discern a spray of the lucky blossom. He rarely put the light and speedy foot wrong or missed a chance to please.

It was after the death of Prince Albert that he became

more than one of the staff. He was sent for to console the young widow at Osborne and with him he brought the favourite pony Lochnagar. He became an escort in foreign travel; then, when back at Balmoral, he could still be the hero on awkward, even dangerous, occasions. On October 7, 1863, a journey was made up Glen Muick by carriage and, after a modest lunch of broth and boiled potatoes, an excursion was made on horseback southwards towards Glen Clova. The subsequent return in the darkness from Loch Muick turned out to be calamitous. The driver Smith "seemed to be quite confused," and it is fair enough to assume that he liked something more consoling than broth and boiled potatoes on such an outing and had brought his flask to the party. He lost the way in the dark and drove so badly that he got the carriage on to very rough ground; at last it was completely overturned with the passengers inside.

Of course, it was John Brown who jumped from the toppling vehicle and rescued the ladies when it crashed; it was John Brown who sensibly cut the traces to release the horses, adroitly produced some claret from the wreck, and promptly sent the wretched Smith back on foot to procure ponies. Finally, after a long wait partially relieved by the claret, the company was able to ride home. It must have been a strange sight, this tumbled party crouching in an overturned vehicle, for Princess Alice had with her a small negro page called Willem. The Queen was bruised and needed nourishment and first aid. " Took only a little soup and fish in my room and had my head bandaged " was the end of the story as she related it in her *Journal*. Once more John Brown had been the hero. Smith, it need hardly be added, did not stay longer in the Queen's service. Mr.

Gladstone was in residence at Balmoral at the time, but his consolation was not sought. Smith was not forgiven and went. Brown was the more esteemed for his part in clearing up after the accident.

The photographs of the period give him a strong, handsome, lively face. His eyes, like those of Robert Burns, were described as dark and gleaming. The legends, as well as the Queen's testimony, indicate that he could be an amusing companion as well as an admirable servant. The Brown mythology contains many reports of a curt wit in the provision of replies to the wearisome or the troublesome. The Queen had always been ready for laughter. Staying, during one of the Great Expeditions, at an inn where the food was scanty and bad, she made this curious comment on the dreary diet and ensuing evening, " No pudding and no fun." One can easily imagine that to one used to the conventional discourse that surrounds a throne, it was fun to have a servant who would make sardonic comment on fools and bores and butters-in. With John Brown about, cheerfulness broke in, even during the dark years of mourning. In 1865 the Queen " appointed that excellent Highlander of mine to attend me always "; her reasons were that he was so unlike a servant, being " so cheerful and attentive."

In a period when respect for the throne was by no means general and even titled folk and important Parliamentarians could be openly Republican, there was obvious matter here for innuendo and scandal-mongering. *Punch*, as a Radical organ, did not shrink from parodying the Court Circular and describing Mr. John Brown as one of the Personages at Balmoral " pleased to listen to the pipes," after eating haggis and before retiring early. The audacity and vulgarity of some other attacks were unlimited. In our present state of opinion about the monarchy it is difficult to believe that sneers could go so far and cartoons extend from candid comment to flagrant cruelty. In 1866, a picture had just been painted by Landseer of the Queen in her widow's weeds mounted on her pony at Osborne with John Brown at the bridle. A paper called *The Tomahawk* published a cartoon of this and actually gave it the caption " All is black that is not Brown "; another of its illustrations showed the Highlander lounging against an empty throne. While the Press (or some of it) was being thus free in comment, John Brown continued to make enemies at Court by his own freedom of speech. What was " fun " for the Queen could be infuriating to her family and the officers of the Household.

The last hope for Brown's good name with the public lay in the chance of becoming a public hero. This opportunity was conveniently provided by a neurotic, half-demented Irishman called Arthur O'Connor. He was a devotee of the Fenians and supported their policy of national liberation by violence. When the Queen was driving into the grounds of Buckingham Palace on February 27, 1872, this crazy creature, who had prepared a Charter of Release for the Fenian prisoners, forced his way to the Royal carriage in order to compel a signature of his document. He even put a pistol to the Queen's head. Brown jumped down from the rumble, snatched the pistol, and held down the man. It was subsequently discovered that O'Connor's weapon was unloaded and that the whole assault was more a piece of bluff than a brutal outrage. But Brown could not know that and he had behaved, in public view, as the gallant guardian. O'Connor was gallant too. He might have pleaded insanity, but he did, in fact, not only plead guilty but added a wish that he had been able to succeed in the assassination. His sentence was a flogging and one year's hard labour.

John Brown's reward for his action in this case, in addition to the still greater favour of his Royal employer, was some mitigation of public criticism; the man from Balmoral, it seemed, might have his uses after all. He demonstrated these still further on a similar occasion a year before his death in 1883. This time the pistol was loaded, and assassination was not so far away. The assailant, Roderick Maclean, had been waiting outside Windsor Station for the arrival of the Queen's train. He fired at her when, having left the station, she was entering her carriage. Brown, already on the rumble, once again made a leap and held his prisoner. Maclean was more sensible and more fortunate than O'Connor. He managed to get himself pronounced insane. The event further helped Brown to be in much better esteem with the nation when he died than when he was in the prime of life.

His death, brought about by erysipelas following a chill, was recorded in the *Court Circular* which *Punch* had parodied nearly twenty years before. " The melancholy event," it was written, " had caused the deepest regret to the Queen and to all members of the Royal Household." His promotions from ghillie to personal attendant in Scotland (1858), to constant personal attendant on all occasions (1864), and to the more recent title of Esquire, were related. John Brown's body lay in his apartment at Windsor Castle for two days and was then removed for burial at Crathie kirkyard. The Queen and Empress Eugénie placed wreaths on the coffin as it was carried from the Castle on the Thames to rest in the grave beside the Dee.

The Queen's wreath was called "a tribute of loving, grateful and everlasting friendship and affection from his honest, best, and most faithful friend." On the granite headstone set over the grave in Crathie John Brown was called "Personal Attendant and Beloved Friend of Queen Victoria," and this quotation was added:

"That friend on whose fidelity you count, that friend given you by circumstances over which you have no control, is God's own gift."

So his parents should have called him Theodore, since that means the gift of God.

Such were the last salutes made to a servant by the monarch of the United Kingdom and its Colonies and Empress of India. Victoria did not hesitate to make public declaration of her intense private sorrow. The boy from Bridgend of Bush had certainly gone as far as might be, laughed at and loathed by many, but deeply valued by one to whom he had seemed the fountain of cheerfulness as well as the pillar of constancy in service. In the grounds of Balmoral his memory was sustained by Boehm's bronze statue and further enshrined in a hilltop cairn. Many replicas of Boehm's work were distributed; Brown's little gifts to the Queen were especially treasured by her after his death. On Boehm's sculpture was engraved a verse beginning "Friend more than servant, Loyal, truthful, brave." The lines were written by the Poet Laureate on command. At Osborne, too, there was tribute; in the grounds a large granite garden-seat proclaimed to the Isle of Wight the virtues of the man from Crathie.

In his life of Queen Victoria, E. F. Benson attributed to "private information" the statement that the Queen, being

greatly pleased by the public reception of her second volume
called *More Leaves from the Journal of a Life in the Highlands*,
was planning a third volume in which the life of John Brown
was to take a chief place. The Dean of Windsor, Randall
Davidson, future Archbishop of Canterbury, was naturally
appalled at the impact on public opinion of such a book,
which might perhaps be written in a highly emotional style,
with more regard to the outpouring of the heart than to the
discreet maintenance of a steady head. So he applied all his
tact to arguing the authoress out of her rash purpose.
Caution, backed by good counsel, did prevail. " After a
long silence of deep displeasure, in which he (Davidson)
wondered whether he had better resign the Deanery, she
sent for him again, talked to him with her usual freedom and
confidence, and no more was heard of Volume Three."[1]
Benson's family connections with the Church add authenti-
city to this report; he had excellent sources and would
never have printed such a statement as this without being
certain of his facts.

India replaced Scotland in close attendance on Her
Majesty. As Empress she thought it proper to study
Oriental tongues and her tutor was an Indian servant,
Munshi Abdul Karim. " Henceforth and till the end of
her life she was waited on by Indian servants; one pushed
her wheeled chairs down the corridors and stood behind her
at lunch and dinner; whether at Balmoral or Windsor or
Osborne, Munshi Abdul Karim gave her daily lessons in
Hindustani. At Windsor he lived in Frogmore Cottage.
Other Indian attendants occupied St. John's Tower where
they were allowed to kill and cook fowls with their native
rites. A smell of blood, onions and curry reminded them of

---

[1] E. F. Benson. *Queen Victoria*, p. 293.

home."[1] A wet week at Balmoral would hardly have done that, but the European attendants upon royalty might have preferred the sharp scent of the dripping conifers to that made by the ingredients of Karim's curry.

"The Munshi" was no more popular with the Household than John Brown had been. He was potentially more dangerous, for Brown, whatever his faults of arrogance, would never have endangered secrets of State obtained by a glance over the royal shoulder or a handling of confidential papers. Ministers may have hated him for his overweening ways; but they could trust his integrity. But Munshi Abdul Karim was a royal companion of a different order. While John Brown's body lay a-mouldering in the grave, his successor, if not his soul, was marching on in a way to which the Scot would scarcely have been sympathetic. The Queen may have had a few lessons in the meaning of Gaelic words from her ghillie, but she was not so close a student of language as she became under the tuition of the Munshi. It is unlikely that the Indian was a popular figure in Upper Deeside.

Two portraits of John Brown have appeared on screen and stage. A film called *The Mudlark* told the tale of a street-urchin who more than once wormed his way into Buckingham Palace and managed to live there for a while as a stow-away. This was based, presumably, on the historical story of The Boy Jones. Young Jones was a tailor's son who first got into the Palace disguised as a chimney-sweep. Two years later he broke in through an open window and spent three days hiding under beds and raiding larders. In the general muddle and administrative jealousies, which Prince Albert found existing "below stairs," such a success for an

[1] E. F. Benson. *Queen Victoria*, p. 311.

invader was made easier. Young Jones claimed to have sat
on the throne and seen and heard much of the Royal Family.
He was more than once sent to prison and more than once
returned to the Palace; he was finally put into the Navy;
this can hardly have been a reward, but rather a hint that
here, at least on the lower deck, was early Victorian Britain's
worst form of incarceration.

The film of *The Mudlark* was post-dated and the un-
biddable boy with a passion for Palace life was shifted from
the eighteen-forties to a later period in which John Brown
could be shown as an arrogant, alcoholic major-domo with
a tendency to fall prone in moments of extreme intoxication.
It was assumed that the Queen displayed a remarkable
capacity for not looking at the floors of the rooms and
passages where Mr. Brown was to be found in one of his
" flat-out " states of collapse. This portraiture of the
Scottish major-domo contributed, no doubt, to the attractions
of the Mudlark's adventures; as a contribution to Palace
history it was possibly an exaggeration of some actual events.
But it does seem to be true that the Queen was, on some
occasions, an adept at looking the other way should her
favourite be over-merry or completely fuddled. Once,
during a Highland excursion, Brown was sent for after
dinner by the Queen, and the report was made that he was
" bashful." In my boyhood, while staying in Banffshire, the
same adjective was used to explain the inability of a gamekeeper, famed for his sword dancing, to perform after our
supper. There had been " merriment " below and he was
" bashful." Was this a special term used in North-East
Scotland to hint politely at intoxication?

A much more sympathetic picture occurs in one of
Laurence Housman's short plays in the series known as

Victoria Regina. These pieces were originally banned by the Censor, but a licence for public performance was granted in 1937. They were very successfully produced as a composite programme in London at the Lyric Theatre in that year, after enjoying great popularity in New York. John Brown is there seen in *An Episode of Home Life in the Highlands.* The year is 1877, and Disraeli has come to take up residence as Minister-in-Attendance at Balmoral. Brown tells the Queen that Disraeli, on his first arrival, had put a tip into his (Brown's) hand; with an air of dignity Brown reacted to this by informing the Prime Minister that he had taken a liberty. " Well, Mr. Brown," said Disraeli, " I've made a mistake, but I don't take it back again." " Very nice and sensible," says the Queen. " And indeed it was, Ma'am," answers Brown. The rugged Highland palm did not vulgarly itch, but it was not altogether averse to oil.

The monarch and her man talk easily and amusingly about the various political visitors, especially about Gladstone and Disraeli. The servant is shown to be the cheerful companion and there is no mention of whisky. There is plausibility in Housman's characterisation of John Brown and assessment of his position. He makes the Personal Servant's privileged position intelligible because Brown as a man has been made reasonably likeable. The Queen found him amusing as well as ever ready in service, and he can hardly have been only the boor and the bully that hostile gossip depicted.

Yet it was a great relief to many when he died. He had few friends in the Royal Family and there are stories of drastic removal of the Boehm statues and other mementoes after the death of the Queen herself. It was an open secret that King Edward VII had disliked the ghillie who, so light or foot, led him up the Cairngorms in his boyhood, had later been his mother's personal counsellor in matters which he, Bertie, thought to be no concern of a servant, however "personal," and had, according to report, even concerned himself with the behaviour and the discipline of the royal children.

Much has been said against John Brown's conduct in later life. "Peremptory and rude, far too fond of whisky, intolerable to visitors at Balmoral and Osborne, patting visitors on the back and being odiously familiar to the family"—that is one side of the picture, as E. F. Benson painted it. He then went on to admit that Brown was a link with the Prince Consort and all the bliss of the first Balmoral years and the "Great Expeditions." The Queen was subject to much advice, possibly conflicting, from people she did not care about. So the confident assumption of command, by a man she liked, an assumption which others so much resented in a rough and hirsute ghillie from the glen, was what delighted his royal mistress. In her distaste for Gladstone with his verbosity in counsel and his public-meeting manner, she could relish a servant who would silence that Voice of God and of the People when in full flow by his curt interjection, "You've said enough."

Lytton Strachey adds a psychological explanation of the Queen's happiness in subjection to a servant:

"The eccentricity appeared to be extraordinary; but, after all, it is no uncommon thing for an autocratic dowager to allow some trusted indispensable servant to adopt towards her an attitude of authority which is jealously forbidden to relatives or friends; the power of a dependant still remains, by a psychological sleight-of-hand, one's own power, even when it is exercised over oneself. When Victoria meekly obeyed the abrupt commands of her henchman to get off her pony or put on her shawl, was she not displaying, and in the highest degree, the force of her volition? People might wonder; she could not help that; this was the manner in which it pleased her to act, and there was an end of it."

It is not difficult to visualise the Queen's position after Albert's death. She had a very high view of the Sovereign's office and was not ready to accept the facts and phrases of democracy as they are accepted now. She was eager to be firm with her statesmen, to speak and act with authority, to make and voice decisions. But how exhausting that can be and how comforting, therefore, when affairs of State have been settled, to lean back at times and let somebody else make the personal resolutions, give the domestic orders, and adopt the peremptory tones! It was nice to be flattered and nice also to be treated with firmness.

In her choice of favourites the Queen went to both extremes. She was captivated by the glib Disraeli because he fawned and called her the Faery; she beamed on the brusque John Brown because he scolded and called her (or was said to call her) "Wumman." (Whether he did ever use this word to her face, even in his most thrasonical moments, is doubtful. The Brown Myth, built on hearsay, cannot be taken as a wholly accurate description of his throne-side manner; nor can we accept the "John Brown Stories" as verbatim reports of his conversational idiom and forms of address.) There was no limit to Disraeli's obsequiousness: he had told Matthew Arnold that flattery laid on with a trowel was royalty's taste and he proceeded to follow up his opinion in practice by making flattery royalty's due. " In these expert hands," wrote Strachey, " the trowel seemed to assume the qualities of some lofty masonic symbol and to be the ornate and glittering vehicle of verities unrealised by the profane." After the tedious diet of Gladstonian rhetoric, here, as Disraeli served it, was a sumptuous banquet for the feminine ear. But, after many banquets, it is an agreeable change to encounter rough and simple fare. The man from Crathie was there to dispense it, and Disraeli had the good sense to leave the Faery with her faith in her Honest John untarnished and undiminished.

It has been suggested that the Queen regarded John Brown almost as a medium and believed that through him the voice of Albert came from beyond. Certainly she was interested in spiritualism, and had some sessions with a medium called Lees. No disgrace in that. Some of the finest Victorian minds were much concerned with messages " from beyond," including that of F. W. H. Myers. Only a few deplorable scientists or ribald Swinburnian poets with vine leaves in their hair, as the Court would have seen them, doubted personal survival after death; by that Court Lord Tennyson's " In Memoriam " was accepted as the poem of poems. To a widow whose devotion to her lost husband was supreme in all her thoughts and feelings the idea of communication with the beloved one who had passed over was quite natural. If the Queen was so far influenced by the rugged integrity of her outspoken Highlander as to overlook his obvious faults of conduct, it is possible that she may have seen in John Brown at least some kind of receiving station for ultra-mundane intimations. Strachey says definitely that she believed that the spirit of Albert was nearer when Brown was near. But this is by no means the same as to claim for Brown a mediumship enjoying direct communion with the dead.

Something of this mysticism there may have been, though Brown, with the gruff common sense and his early taste for merriment in the Commercial Room amid the clink of glasses, hardly seems to be the kind of Highlander who would possess a natural gift of spiritual privileges. It is said that something in the Highland air gives the man of the glens the doubtful blessing of "second sight," which appears mainly to be a melancholy power to foresee deaths. There is always a tendency to credit the inhabitants of wild and lonely country with faculties denied to the common man of the crowded city, but Brown does not seem, at least in the light of history, to have been a possessor of exceptional gifts or a creature visited by special enlightenment. More would be known about this, no doubt, if his diaries had not been impounded by Sir Henry Ponsonby and destroyed with the Queen's approval.

The picture of a domineering major-domo, a picture almost inevitable in the case of John Brown, sets one thinking of Malvolio. It is a curious coincidence that immediately after Brown's death in 1883 there were three major productions of *Twelfth Night* in Central London; two were in the same year, one at the Gaiety with the young Beerbohm Tree as Malvolio, and the other at the Strand with Edward Compton and Virginia Bateman: in the summer of 1884 Irving and Ellen Terry produced their version of the Illyrian comedy at the Lyceum. Some London playgoers can hardly have failed to think of the dead Highlander when they heard the recital of a steward's self-love, and of his "stubborn and uncourteous parts," so long had these been the gossip of London. Had not Brown "put himself in the trick of singularity," been "opposite" with the kinsmen of the Queen, and surly with strangers and servants? No doubt, on occasion, he had. Exemplary in youth, he had failed in later life " to carry corn," as they say, and he signally failed, it seems, to carry his liquor.

But there is much to be put forward on the man's behalf. In his early years of service he must have behaved extremely well to have been so much esteemed by the Prince Consort as well as by the Queen. After the death of Albert, his distraught widow turned to the servant and tried him too high and too hard. He was increasingly encouraged to be audacious, to give orders, to be a prop. It is small wonder that he at last put himself in the trick of singularity, with a Malvolian relish in the greatness thrust upon him. He might have taken the accident of grandeur with more humility when he was out of the Queen's presence; but he was a self-made man; he could now pay for any rebuffs which he had suffered (or fancied that he had suffered) from the gentlemen of the Court, or the junior members of the Royal Family. He could be a somebody, as it were, the moor-cock turned peacock. He could assert his unique position of favour and of trust. When a servant knows that he is very popular with his employer and very unpopular with his employer's friends and relations, the temptation to play the former strength against the latter weakness must be very great. John Brown was not proof against temptation nor, having surrendered to it, was he a master of tact.

But I cannot believe that he was really the appalling boor whose picture has been created by the John Brown legend. The legend was built, at least in part, on the hearsay of jealous, affronted, and class-conscious people. "Simple-minded, kind-hearted, and disinterested." Those were the

Queen's considered words and, though she may have shut one eye to much, she was not so short-sighted in general as to be completely misled. These adjectives are a complete contradiction of the legend's portrait of a jumped-up megalomaniac. My own guess, which may, of course, be attributed to the loyalty and regard for a family name, is that Laurence Housman's Brown is a reasonably accurate sketch. The groom had risen, on his deserts, to be the candid friend, and candour, from one pair of lips, was a welcome change in the conversations of the Queen. He provided a salty kind of comment, he amused, and he took command when command was obviously needed; he was a bachelor with one thought only, to be completely at the service of the one person who had raised him up. Completely? There were occasions when he had to plead " indisposition " or, as he said in his younger days, " bashfulness." But, on the whole, his devotion was beyond question and attested by some courageous grappling with the would-be assassins. Moreover, good manners are more common than bad ones in the Highlanders and certainly young John from Crathie would have started out with an asset of politeness.

Brown was protective and we have to remember that there are frequently some stray, demented people who think that royalty is the cause of all their troubles. The Queen had not only to expect an occasional lunatic assault; she had to endure threats and rumours of still more assaults. Mythical they usually were, but it was hardly pleasant to have the hint in 1867 that two whole shiploads of would-be assassins had embarked from New York in order to make an end of herself and of most of Britain's high-and-mighty ones. They were, of course, legendary figures and their raid upon Osborne never happened. But the warning had come

BIRKHALL

ABERGELDIE CASTLE

QUEEN VICTORIA AND JOHN BROWN AT BALMORAL, 1868

from lofty circles and was far from comfortable hearing. Great precautions were taken, so much so that the Sovereign considered that the official arrangements left her a prisoner. What effectively consoled her was the constant presence of the loyal Highlander who after all did prove his prowess at the pistol's end.

Moreover, he did much more than exercise surveillance: he poured out sympathy. The age of tears had not passed; grown men, even the seemingly rugged Highlanders, could weep to admiration, and John Brown was ever ready with his plentiful compassion. The sardonic have suggested that what the Queen really saw was the rheumy eye of the alcoholic rather than the moisture of true mourning. Brown served her as a frequent messenger of calamity and never failed to carry an announcement of death in a discreet and moving way. It was Brown who had to tell her that the Keeper of the Privy Purse, Sir Thomas Biddulph, " so wonderfully unselfish and disinterested a man " had died at Abergeldie in 1878. Brown, in the following year, brought to the Queen's room the dreadful news that " The Young French Prince is killed." This was the young Prince Imperial, killed by a Zulu ambush. " Poor dear Empress, her only, only child—her all gone." The Queen wrote that she was " beside herself " and " Brown so distressed " was consolingly beside her too. Why should he not be? He was a human being of human sympathies, and he came of a race whose pipe-music is rich in lamentation. The idea of a lachrymose humbug has pleased the cynical, but it need not be accepted as the whole truth.

It is a striking fact that General Ponsonby, who had little liking for Brown and found him coarse and domineering— one hardly expects a General to care for a swollen-headed sergeant-major—did, in the end, concede him a good deal. After the funeral of the Personal Attendant in 1883, Ponsonby wrote: " Wreaths from Princesses, Empresses and Ladies-in-Waiting are lying on Brown's grave. He was the only person who would fight and make the Queen do what she did not wish. He did not always succeed nor was his advice always the best. But I believe he was honest, and with all his want of education, his roughness, his prejudices and other faults he was undoubtedly a most excellent servant to her."[1]

Sir Francis Knollys, later, as Viscount Knollys, private secretary to King Edward VII, observed, " I presume all the Family will rejoice at his death, but I think very probably they are short-sighted." It was conceded by Brown's enemies that he was honest and loyal—or at least too stupid to do any profitable peeping and spying.

The Queen's favour, it is usually surmised, was due in great measure to Albert's regard for Brown as a servant in the home and as an ally in the difficult business of mastering British blood-sports. But there was probably more in her addiction to the ghillie than the widow's respect for a dear husband's favourite. Surely the value of John Brown, in her eyes, was his embodiment of a place, *the* place, " this dear Paradise." When he came to Osborne or Windsor or London, he was Balmoral; he brought Deeside with him; he was the river and the hill where Albert had been in frequent ecstasies and all had been perfection. If he drank— well, the Queen had supped (and enjoyed) the good Scottish whisky in the cottages at Crathie and had been much comforted with a flask from her ghillie's hand during the ardours and endurances of the Great Expeditions. John Brown, if

---

[1] *Henry Ponsonby* by Arthur Ponsonby, p. 128.

he had any taste for a rhyme, might have enjoyed Charles
Murray's defence of a Donside figure, Tam the Miller, a
dusty and a thirsty fellow:

> " *An' sae, man, I canna help thinkin'*
> *The neighbours unkindly; in truth,*
> *Afore they can judge o' my drinkin'*
> *They first maun consider my drooth.*"

In moments when Brown's behaviour had been embarrassing, his lenient Queen might also have smiled at those
excusing lines. He had a drooth (thirst) and she knew it.

She was always yearning to get back to Scotland. What
better sign of her affection than the fact that she spent seven
years of her life in that country—if we add up the weeks of
her various visitations? Since there had, every year, to be
those desolating days of autumn parting from the murmurs
of the Dee below the Castle and from the view of Lochnagar
above the western woods, it was consoling to have about her,
always about her, a man who spoke with the Aberdeenshire
speech and could bring into an English State Room the tang
of the air in the Ballochbuie forest and on the Braes of Mar.
It was the practice that in England he remained Scottish,
kilted and bonneted. His function, which he performed to
full satisfaction, was to be national and to provide a cure for
the Queen's Deeside nostalgia. He was to stand like a
lonely Scottish fir from the Caledonian forest amid the
gentler plantations in the Great Park of Windsor: he was
to be the abiding thistle on the trim lawns of Buckingham
Palace.

CHAPTER EIGHT

The Kirk

THE kirk of Crathie has become a favourite place of public resort for Sunday sightseers; it can be viewed quietly from within on other days; as a piece of history, as well as an example of modern church architecture, it deserves the travellers' pause. For many hundreds of years there have been gatherings there for sacred, as well as secular, purposes. Ever since the days of the early Celtic Church there has been Christian worship in and around Balmoral and long before the coming of the Christian missionaries men raised their stones of dedication where they buried their dead in stone " kists."

There is a pool in the Dee, opposite the grounds of Balmoral Castle, known as Polmanaire; this is generally explained as the water dedicated to the local saint; it is the pool of Manirus or Manaire, of whom it is recorded that " he travelled painfully among the Highlanders in the upper parts of Mar that he might recover them from the many remainders of idolatry and superstition which, even till then, were to be found among them." This use of the word " painfully " does not mean that he suffered from sore feet or climatic exposure, but simply that he took pains in the

164

sense of trouble. A preacher in Scotland could be described as a painful speaker without offence; it was not implied that he inflicted agony; he was just an industrious and conscientious worker in the pulpit.

The Saint had a heritage of paganism around, but not altogether against, him. The Church was sensible and practical; it would not destroy the old rituals and the ceremonial sites; by doing so it would give offence; it could absorb them, working by persuasion and substitution. Aberdeenshire has a plentiful supply of Stone Age relics and even so remote and barren a region as the Braes of Mar has its spoor of the neolithic men and their successors who made their mark with pillars and circles. I have mentioned the Standing Stone at Abergeldie Castle. The church or chapel of St. Manaire is associated with a knoll near Rhynabaich on the north side of the river nearly half-way between Crathie and Ballater. Here there is a Standing Stone, and Stirton recalls with some doubts the tradition that the officiating priest used to put his Bible upon this handy monolith because it was part of the Chapel. Stirton adds " more likely it was the spot where some prehistoric burial had taken place." Why the alternative? The Church could take over a sacred spot or burial ground from paganism and use it for its own purposes.

That this was done at Inverey is suggested by the fact that there was once there a " Chappell of the Seven Maidens." This name has not a Christian ring to it, whereas it certainly has a neolithic one. In many parts of Britain the Stone Circles are known as the Maidens and the remains are frequently seven or thereabouts in number. It is surely a fair guess that the " Chappell " at Inverey was an adaptation or building wrought out of an old stone circle? It would have made things far easier for St. Manaire in his painful travellings if he could convert the aboriginals by turning their shrines to the service of the new God instead of enraging them by contempt of the old and by the uprooting of stones long held to be sacred. But many superstitions were hard to kill. During a Christian burial hand-bells were rung in order to frighten away the evil spirits that might be infiltrating the cemetery. Supposed witches were hunted and even burned in North-East Scotland until well into the eighteenth century.

" Chappells " were numerous in the early days of Christianity in this area. They must have been quite small and primitive places since they were provided in such ample number. Crathie had four besides a Parish Church, including one at " Balmurrel " and another at Micras, (Micras is an odd name. Presumably it can be explained in terms of Gaelic, but it might also be a hint, since this was a religious site, of an old link with Mithras, the eastern sun-god. This cult from the Mediterranean coasts and the Near East could have been spread by earlier travellers than the Romans, that is by the explorers of the Bronze and Iron Age whose marks are all over Aberdeenshire.) Queen Victoria with her eagerness to remember her husband and her family with cairns, obelisks and pyramidal structures was conforming unconsciously to the earliest practices of her country-side; she was setting up the Standing Stone whereby the fallen and the prostrate person was given (or assisted to) immortality. It is impossible to draw hard or firm lines between one religious cult and another; the Kirk of Crathie, whither now the sightseers flock on August and September Sundays, is the last in a line of sacred stones which go back into the pre-history of Deeside. There is a material, as well as a spiritual, relevance in the saying, " Upon this rock I will build my church." As kirks began to centralise the work of the little dispersed chapels, Crathie became a " Kirkton," small though it was.

Until 1878 Crathie and Braemar had been a single parish, but an enormous one. The growth of Braemar, to which the royal occupation of Balmoral had contributed, made a division necessary. We know that there had been separate churches for a long time. Crathie had some distinguished Ministers during the seventeenth and eighteenth centuries: Adam Ferguson, a good scholar and teacher and father of a famous historian, was one, and Murdoch McLennan another. The latter was a poet, or at least a rhymer. His long piece on the Battle of Sheriffmuir begins:

> " *There's some say that we wan,*
> *And some say that they wan,*
> *And some say that nane wan at a', man;*
> *But ae thing I'm sure,*
> *That at Sheriff-muir*
> *A battle there was, that I saw, man;*
> *And we ran, and they ran; and they ran, and we ran;*
> *And we ran, and they ran awa, man."*

It continues without more inspiration for a long time. Some of it, sung at a concert with everybody cosy, could pass well enough. But when one sees his work in cold print, the Crathie Minister is hardly to be ranked as an important bard.

The Scottish Church discipline of the eighteenth century was very severe. Sabbath-breaking, brawling, and adultery or ante-nuptial fornication could bring severe and even barbarous penalties. There were the " jougs " outside the church, iron collars more uncomfortable and humiliating than the stocks. A "jouged" malefactor would have to stand the raillery of the supposedly righteous lookers-on. There would also be commands to appear at kirk in sackcloth and to take the conspicuous Stool of Repentance under the pulpit and there accept rebuke. The sermons then delivered were not, it seems, of the grave and logical kind that one now expects of the Scottish Kirk, but highly emotional, rather in the Welsh manner. They were also full of menace. " As you comb your head think of your sins which are more than the hairs thereon." This type of command, which the bald could perhaps take with a complacent smile, was typical, at least for the hirsute, of the admonitory pulpiteering manner. The godly had to be considering always their great and countless iniquities and the fiery penalties to come.

The Scottish Ministers, who thus kept Crathie in a lively expectation of hell-fire, did not have large stipends; nor, on the other hand, did they have to preach upon an empty stomach. They were supplied with tithes in kind as well as in cash. To have the porridge laid on and the " flesher " (or butcher) circumvented was certainly something of use. The name of their provided houses hints at a certain quality of construction, if not at splendour. The mansion or manse was well above the village level of building and amenity: the Minister was clothed above the average and he walked, if not as delicately as Agag, at least with solid foundations. Stirton recounts that, when the ordinary folk had only rough deer-skin brogues for their feet, the Minister had the shoemaker from a town to call upon him and equip him with the dignity of properly fashioned shoes. But the Minister had to have the raw materials ready for the " soutar," leather, hemp, rosin, and so on.

The remnants of the pre-Reformation Kirk, which lasted as a place of worship into the nineteenth century, can be seen and inspected in the old Crathie kirkyard. This lies between the north Deeside road and the river itself. There is always some interesting social history in kirkyard masonry and inscriptions. Beside the leafy ruins are several graves of the Farquharsons and the granite tombstones put up by Queen Victoria to her favourite Crathie servants, John Grant and John Brown. In 1731 the building was in great need of repair and £430, an enormous sum in those days for a poor parish to raise, had to be found. It was successfully obtained by a species of property-tax on the Heritors; these were the land-owners of the Parish. Yet, within three-quarters of a century, the mended building was abandoned and, during the long ministry of the Rev. Charles McHardy, it was decided to build afresh and on a different site; this new structure was given a loftier and more commanding stance, above the road instead of in the riverside dip. Mention of the word dip reminds me that the present Minister of Crathie, Mr. Lamb, is (or has been) a round-the-year bather in the Dee. How cold the waters of the Dee can become, as they pour down from the Cairngorm snows, I shiver to think. Mr. Lamb's performance makes the Christmas Day plungers into London's Serpentine seem almost to be sybarites or " softies."

In November, 1803, Mr. McHardy declared the repaired Crathie Kirk to be once more in a ruinous condition. He asked for a new one which would hold 700. Within six months the Presbytery had passed the plans and had resolved to spend £820 on the building, the architects to be William and Andrew Clerk. It was ready for use next year, a simple, whitewashed building with a small belfry: the type is common in Scotland still, an unassuming place for un-assuming people, a logical home for a pulpit where the Word would be logically argued, a plain edifice for plain edification. The pews were very narrow and the worshippers must have been ready to pack in if all 700 were to arrive. The Minister, however, did not hesitate to make some powerful assump-tions: a stone above the doorway carried, as one of three texts, this from the Epistle to the Galatians:

" But there be some that trouble you, and would pervert the gospel of Christ. But though we, or an angel from heaven, preach any other gospel unto you, let him be accursed. For I neither received it of man neither was I taught it but by the revelation of Jesus Christ."

Mr. McHardy was certainly a confident Pauline and ready to deal out damnation. He is described as having been a strong and forceful person, like one carrying authority. He was succeeded by the Rev. Alexander McFarlane in 1822 and Mr. McFarlane was followed in 1840 by the Rev. Archibald Anderson to whom great kindliness of spirit was attributed and also a ready hospitality at the Manse. His preaching was of a simpler and easier kind than that which had been delivered before. It was during his Ministry that the Queen and Prince Consort first came to the church. They mounted the stairs to take their seats in the gallery which ran round three sides of the building. The west side was allocated to Balmoral and Invercauld, the centre to Abergeldie, and the east to Mar Lodge and the house of Monaltrie.

Mr. Anderson called in prominent Scottish preachers to

visit Crathie during royal visits, a practice which continues. The visiting Minister is usually a guest at Balmoral over the week-end. Among the eminent Victorians thus called were Dr. Norman McLeod, Principal Caird, Principal Tulloch, and Dr. Cameron Lees. The Queen recorded that she had never heard anything finer than Dr. McLeod's address in 1854, while next year Principal Caird " electrified all present by a most admirable and beautiful sermon which lasted nearly an hour—as fine as Mr. McLeod's sermon last year—and sent us home much edified." The Prince Consort was a great admirer of Dr. Caird. Mr. Gladstone, when he came up in 1865, had reservations. But Gladstone was annoyed by the absence of an Episcopalian Church. He wrote to his wife:

" Sept. 27.—I do not think Sunday is the best of days here. I in vain inquired with care about episcopal services; there did not seem to be one within fifteen miles, if indeed so near. We had something between family prayer and a service in the dining-room at ten; it lasted about forty minutes. Dr. Caird gave a short discourse, good in material, though over florid in style for my taste. The rest of the day I have had to myself. The Prince and Princess of Hesse I think went to the parish church. You are better off at Penmaenmawr. . . ."

On the following Sunday his distaste for worship outside his own communion was kindly met and he was driven down Deeside to find methods more congenial. He could record that " The service at Ballater has made great difference in favour of this Sunday. It was celebrated in the Free Kirk School Room for Girls and with a congregation most attentive though very small, and no one left the room when we came to Holy Communion. . . . The sermon was extremely good, but the priest had a few antics. I believe that this is about the first expedition ever made from Balmoral to an episcopal service. . . . There was no chaplain here to-day and so no dining-room service, which for many I fear means no service at all."

What with Caird's flowers of rhetoric and the " antics " of the priest in Ballater, Gladstone appeared to suffer on both sides. But a blow against the Kirk had been struck for emancipation and he could proudly claim that " perhaps encouraged by my example, Captain W. got a drag to Castleton (Braemar) this morning, being a Roman." Up the valley, down the valley, anything to avoid Principal Caird in the dining-room and the Scottish service in the Crathie kirk where the Queen and the Prince Consort found deep satisfaction. The Prince, a connoisseur of pulpit eloquence, put Caird second only to Dr. Samuel Wilberforce, Bishop of Oxford, for performance in the pulpit. Precisians could object to the Queen's presence at the Scottish Kirk, since she was Head of the Church of England; but most people nowadays would surely take the broader and more courteous view that the Queen, when in Scotland, a member of the United Kingdom, has a right, or even a duty, to attend the service of its Established Church, an attendance emphasising the Protestant Succession.

There was more complaint when she attended Communion Sunday. She found the occasion " most touching and beautiful," and stated that she was " more moved than she could say." Sacrament Sunday used to occur in Crathie once a year and that at midsummer. It was a day-long convention and a great gathering of far-separated people enjoyed the chance of reunion, driving in early from their crofts in the glens to meet and talk before the sermon began. Mrs. Lindsay has left us a picture of the scene.[1]

"Two long tables, covered with white linen, were arranged across the centre of the church; and such was the number of communicants that these were generally cleared and refilled with fresh occupants four or five times. Just under the pulpit was a small table, also covered with a white cloth, on which were placed the bread and wine. Presiding at this, stood the clergyman who ' served the tables ' as it was called, that is, gave a short address before and after the administration of the Sacrament; and round him were grouped the officiating elders. The communicants entered and left the tables to the strains of that grandest of thanksgiving hymns—the 103rd Psalm, in the beautiful Scottish metrical version, sung to the tune of ' London New.'

"The services lasted five or six hours, and few of the people found them tedious, with the intervals of rest which their arrangement afforded; touchingly solemn and impressive they always appeared to me."

But that some people did find it tedious is shown by the sad case of Isobel Macgregor who in 1720 was " before the session for the breaking of the glass in a window on the day of the Communion. When she was without in the kirk-yard sleeping, her head fell through the window and broke the glass." This must have been extremely painful for the somnolent Isobel Macgregor, but doubtless there was more concern about the material damage done. Stirton remarks gravely of this episode " Glass was very seldom used in those days. Windows were simply wooden shutters or only

[1] *Recollections of a Royal Parish*, p. 104.

half-made of glass. The glassen window was a rare and important feature in the Church."

Soon after the royal occupation of Balmoral the practice of the Kirk was altered and two Communions, in spring and autumn, were substituted for the single midsummer ceremony. The Queen attended the Autumn Communion, which she herself has so vividly described, in November, 1871. But she did not undergo a whole day of celebration. She went to the Kirk at twelve and was home before a quarter to two; there were then many more communicants still waiting. (The Minister was now Dr. Taylor who had succeeded Mr. Anderson. He was much approved and both the Manse and the stipend were improved with the Queen's help.) Dr. Robertson, the Queen's Commissioner, in his office as an Elder, handed her the elements and thereafter she was a regular partaker, little as this pleased the Archbishop of Canterbury and Mr. Gladstone. She had not only a broad mind but a firm will.

Dr. Campbell, from Lonmay in Aberdeenshire, followed Dr. Taylor who went on to be Minister at Morningside in Edinburgh and later was chosen to be Professor of Divinity and Church History in the University of Edinburgh. During Dr. Campbell's time the parish of Crathie and Braemar was divided into two for religious purposes, while it was kept united for civil administration. It was also during his time that the simple, whitewashed kirk of 1805 was considered to be inadequate and the building which visitors see to-day was put in its place. The people of the nineteenth century had a simple faith in Progress, which we, with sufficient reason, have somewhat lost, and Progress, thought Dr. Campbell, must be applied to kirks as well as to secular premises. He expressed his regrets, but ". . . It was felt, however, that the time had arrived when, in obedience to the law of progress, sentimental considerations had to be set aside, and a decided step taken towards improvement. Loyally did all connected with the parish lend their support to the movement when once it was fairly started. But the sacrifice had to be made which attends upon all progress, and it was not without many regretful feelings, and much pulling of heart-strings, that the old and familiar was parted with. The last day on which worship was held in the old church was the 23rd of April, 1893."

The Queen and the other Heritors agreed to the new project. Indeed, she gave it her personal aid in all possible ways, being present both at the laying of the foundation stone in 1893 and at the opening and dedication on 18th June, 1895. The architect was Dr. A. Marshall Mackenzie, who was also responsible for Marischal College, Aberdeen.

In this case Progress, not often a benefactor in the matter of late-Victorian architecture, proved to be a kindly force. People who drive up Deeside expecting to find something in a feebly Gothic mode discover a cross-shaped building made of white granite hewn from the neighbouring quarry of Inver and roofed in terra-cotta tiles. There is a central tower with a small spire: it is a kirk that points to heaven, but does not ambitiously soar there. It is broadly based on the native rock, clean and shining without and cordial within. Various aspects of its pattern and its detail have been attributed to the examples of St. Monance in Fife and to Jedburgh Abbey and Pluscarden Priory. The word apse is defined as " an arched semi-circular or polygonal recess at the east end of the choir of a church," and the apse in this case is semi-circular. The Balmoral pews are on the right and the woodwork carries the Rose, Thistle and Shamrock and the monogram of Queen Victoria. The hexagonal pulpit is made of fifteen varieties of Scottish granite and native Scottish stones have also been used in its construction; Princess Louise, the Duchess of Argyll, presented a collection of stones from the island of Iona which have been worked into the granite. This may sound over-elaborate, but the result to the eye is very pleasing, as also are the Iona marbles of the Communion table, which, with the screen of old English oak carved after the style of that in the renowned King's College Chapel of Aberdeen, is a commemoration gift for the late King placed and unveiled by King George V and Queen Mary in 1911.

Naturally there are many memorials, in the form of busts or stained-glass windows, to the members of the Royal Family. Most moving, perhaps, to students of nineteenth-century history is the monument on the East Wall to "Victoria Adelaide Mary Louise, German Empress and Queen of Prussia, Princess Royal of Great Britain and Ireland." "Vicky," whose courtship in a glen only a few miles away has already been described, had a most unfortunate life. Her husband, who was no typical Prussian, might have counteracted the influence of Bismarck who hated the Daughter of Britain; but the Chancellor fought against both her and the Prince, who only succeeded to the throne when he was a stricken man: he was immediately succeeded by her son, Kaiser William II, who was not only in opposition to the sane policy of his father and mother, but fiery and self-willed. The Princess Royal of Great Britain she at heart remained. She had been the darling of the Prince Consort, for she was clear of mind and a well-educated girl who could talk, even in early youth, on level terms with her father on the intellectual subjects that so much

ROYAL GROUP AT BALMORAL, 1896

(L. TO R. STANDING) Duke of Connaught ; Princess Patricia of Connaught (Lady Patricia Ramsay) ; Prince of Wales (King Edward VII) ; Duchess of Connaught ; Princess Victoria of Schleswig-Holstein (Princess Helena Victoria) ; Prince Charles of Denmark (King Haakon of Norway); Princess Victoria of Wales ; Emperor Nicholas II of Russia ; Princess Margaret of Connaught (Crown Princess of Sweden) (SEATED) Princess of Wales (Queen Alexandra) ; Empress of Russia (Princess Victoria Alice of Hesse) ; Princess Louise, Princess Royal (Duchess of Fife) ; Princess Charles of Denmark (Princess Maud of Wales, later Queen of Norway)

THE ROYAL FAMILY AT BALMORAL, 1960

interested him. But her influence was over-ridden. And so to 1914.

The new kirk, accordingly, with its lofty and beautiful setting amid birch and larch and conifers, is a fitting piece of Scottish fabric. It has become the target of a huge cavalcade of cars on Sundays in late summer and of much peeping and gazing which seems to me foolish and unmannerly, although loyalty can be urged on its behalf. If the weather is fine, people will congregate for hours to see the Queen and her husband drive by in their car. The drone of traffic through the Deeside towns begins early, thanks to those Sabbath day journeys. The habit had started when horse-transport alone was available. Quite a number went from Ballater and Braemar to watch Queen Victoria's carriage with the white horses carry her to worship in the kirk of her affections and her reverence. The building can be properly seen, with proper guidance, on a week-day.

After the Disruption of 1843 the Free Church people gathered to worship in a barn lent by Dr. Robertson. His daughter, Mrs. Lindsay, has confessed to enjoying some disputatious theology through open windows on a summer's day from a niche among the garden-bushes outside. Later a kirk was built on the Abergeldie property and the foundation stone was laid by Lord Dalhousie with an additional sermon by the great Dr. Guthrie of Edinburgh. What would Gladstone have thought if the Queen had elected to attend services there? His liberalism did not extend to his theology. More recently another Free Kirk and Manse were built about a mile below Balmoral.

There are many tales of the second Crathie kirk, the austere but well-loved building visited by Queen Victoria during the main part of her residence at Balmoral. The first of her Crathie Ministers, Mr. Anderson, had a collie who was a regular follower of the Sunday service. He followed the Minister up the pulpit steps and lay quietly at the top during the sermon, or quietly at least until he deemed that time was up and further eloquence unnecessary. Then, Mrs. Lindsay relates, he would rise, stretch himself, and yawn. When the Queen first came, Mr. Anderson left the dog at home, but she heard of the collie's habits, had seen a sketch of the pulpit with him lying there, and suggested that he must certainly not be excluded for her sake. Although she was a ready absorber of sermons, especially of Scottish ones, she may have valued the animal's services as time-keeper.

Then there was a great character in Wee Jamie Gow who " howked the holes " (dug the graves) in the kirkyard. Being so small he was afraid of falling in and is said to have scanted the spadework; also, when he rang the church bell, his tiny frame was in danger of being carried into mid-air as he hauled powerfully away to greet the Minister coming across from the Manse. It is commonly believed, with some justice, that modern ways of life flatten out the oddities of human character and that even remote places no longer have their pack of " cards," but only the same card repeated fifty-two times. That is probably less true of rural Scotland than of most areas and the individuals of curious wit and of racy humour who appear in the Balmoral legends may have left worthy descendants. I have been told by one who has been a guest at Balmoral that the stalker allotted to him for a day on the hills stopped suddenly in the midst of their operations and said, " What do you think, sir, was the meanest thing ever done? " Obviously the answer to this gigantic query had to be awaited. " It was done, sir, by the ventriloquist who threw a man's voice under an old maid's bed." With this entertainment given, the stalker applied himself to the day's business. Queen Victoria might not have been amused. But this is to move rather far from Church affairs. Still, the Jamie Gows were a large part and parcel of Crathie and its kirk, and seem to be not yet extinct.

CHAPTER NINE

Stroll of Players

THE place of Deeside in theatrical history is ancient and distinguished, at least as far as the coastal city of Aberdeen is concerned. It is even possible that William Shakespeare was there himself, though it is difficult to see how he fitted in constant writing if he was much, and distantly, on tour—as many of his fellows of the Lord Chamberlain's, later the King's, troupe were.

The facts, which are documented in the civic records of Aberdeen as well as of London, are these. In October, 1601, the King's Servants, " who play comedies and stage plays " were recommended by a special letter of King James VI of Scotland, later James I of England, to the Dean of Guild of the city of Aberdeen. They were paid for their performances out of civic funds and were also entertained to a " sopper that nicht thaye plaiid to the toune." Even greater favour was shown, either as a matter of policy or in genuine approbation, to the King's favourites. Laurence Fletcher, " comedian servitor " to the King, was admitted along with several gentlemen of birth to the freedom of the city, a remarkable recognition for a strolling player. Fletcher may have been a Scot in origin and so may have started with King James on his side. Certainly he went to London later.

Soon after the accession of James to the English throne, he headed the official list of the King's Men with Shakespeare's name second to his. This was in the royal licence granted to this company, " freely to use the Arts and Facultie of playing as well for the Recreation of our loveinge Subjects as for our Solace and Pleasure when we shall thinke goode to see them." This licence was granted to the company, not only at " the Globe within our Countie of Surrey but in any Universitie, Towne or Boroughe whatsoever within our said Realm and Dominions."

Fletcher was therefore an important person in his craft as well as an honorary Burgess of Aberdeen. It is most unfortunate that the civic records in Aberdeen do not mention the play then given or the names of the players (other than Fletcher) who were recommended to the Dean of Guild by King James in the autumn of 1601. But it is definitely stated that they were English and this, together with the presence of Fletcher, later to be so important among the King's Men, does suggest that the team of strolling players in Aberdeen was Shakespeare's own " fellowship " —the " Lord Chamberlain's Men " as they were still called while Queen Elizabeth was alive.

They had good reason to keep clear of London in the autumn of 1601. This was particularly true of Shakespeare. He was the author of *Richard II*, the performance of which play about a monarch deposed had been specially arranged and specially rewarded with double pay by the partakers in the abortive Essex Rebellion of that spring. The Privy Council gravely took note of the performance which was arranged to take place before the rising, and the players were in serious danger, when Essex was beheaded and Southampton sent to the Tower with a life-sentence.

A long tour was obviously tactful when noble heads were rolling on Tower Hill. So the Players at Aberdeen in October of 1601, giving a performance more or less commanded by the Scottish King, were, quite probably, Shakespeare's fellows. It is a fair guess—and no more than a guess —that Shakespeare may have been there, and that during these travels he was acquiring that interest in early Scottish history, early Scottish witchcraft, the climate of Inverness and the whereabouts of Forres, which was later on to be manifest in *Macbeth*.

Since, in October, the great gathering of Lairds and Tinchels for hunting in the Braes of Mar would be over, some of the gentry may by then have turned citywards and patronised in Aberdeen the English players so dear to their own king. There were distinguished French visitors in the town at the time and the social life must have been brisk. It would be nice to think that the players were also " commanded " to play in one of the Deeside castles, as their successors were later to be commanded to appear at Balmoral. But we have no news of that. Still, they did reach old Aberdeen, with royal support.

We must jump nearly three centuries before we reach a further link of the monarchy with the players in Aberdeenshire. In England there were Command Performances during the reign of Queen Victoria; these had begun at Windsor Castle in 1848. The play then chosen was *The Merchant of Venice* with Mr. and Mrs. Charles Kean appearing as Shylock and Portia. It was not the accepted thing at that time for royalty to attend the public theatres and, since the Queen enjoyed the drama provided on this occasion, there were, after such a successful experiment, a number of further requests for what the first of the Stuart Kings of

England had called Solace and Pleasure. Among the leaders of the stage thus honoured with demands for their services were Benjamin Webster and Samuel Phelps, the great Shakespearean of Sadler's Wells, in addition to Kean. After the death of the Prince Consort and the Queen's retirement into her long mourning the custom of " commanding " naturally ceased. To the respectable Victorians a play was a play and mourning was mourning. A visit even to *Hamlet* would have been held unseemly in the early years of grief. In the Queen's case those years ran into decades.

For the renewal we have to turn to Deeside. On October 1, 1881, the Prince of Wales, always fond of the theatre, entertained Mr. Edgar Bruce and his company at Abergeldie Castle. The Queen came over for the evening from Balmoral; it was her first visit to a theatrical entertainment since her husband's death. The play was *The Colonel*, a piece adapted by Burnand from a French comedy and we may presume that it was not of a severe quality, likely to demand the exercise of higher thought, or such as to challenge critical faculties in the Prince and his guests after a day's shooting and an evening's dinner. We may also presume that Mr. Bruce and the players engaged were then making a tour in Scotland and so were fetched in from one of their " dates " and not specially carried all the way from London. *The Colonel* enjoyed a long run, appropriately, at the Prince of Wales's Theatre in London: the favour of the first royal command, after so long a discontinuance of these requests, must have been a useful advertisement.

Ten years later came song and dance, to both of which the young Queen had been so partial in youth. The D'Oyly Carte Company was commanded to bring *The Mikado* to

Balmoral. This must have been the first professional performance under this roof. It must also have been a ticklish occasion. To accommodate an orchestra and to present an operatic (or operettic) company in a ballroom of such limited size as that at Balmoral must have needed ingenious planning of the platform and deft stage management. But greater was still to come. Two years later Sir Squire and Lady Bancroft and Sir John Hare, all at the top of reputation, appeared at Balmoral in Sardou's *Diplomacy*. Their revival of this strong drama had been presented and much approved at the Garrick Theatre in London in February of that year. As a very effective example of what Bernard Shaw called " Sardoodledom " it has been frequently brought back to the stage and rarely fails to please. Undoubtedly the Balmoral house-party could hardly have had a more accomplished company to commend to the august audience its " powerful situations."

In September, 1894, Beerbohm Tree, better known later as Sir Herbert Tree, was requested to bring his productions of two plays, *The Red Lamp* and *The Ballad Monger*. The former was a very popular piece by Outram Tristan which had been repeatedly revived at the Haymarket in London since its first presentation at the Comedy in 1887. The latter, an adaptation from the French by Walter Besant and W. H. Pollock, had been its fairly constant companion in an evening's bill.

The last of the professional artists invited to Balmoral were Mr. George Alexander (later Sir George) and the distinguished members of his St. James's Theatre Company. The command to them came in mid-September, 1895, when the Queen was seventy-six years old. Alexander was touring seven plays at once, which must have meant a strenuous life for his stage-managers. These included, along with two forgotten pieces, *The Second Mrs. Tanqueray* by Pinero, *The Importance of Being Earnest* by Oscar Wilde, *The Triumph of the Philistines* by Henry Arthur Jones, *The Idler* by Haddon Chambers, and *Liberty Hall* by R. C. Carton. Obviously, after the scandal in the spring, Wilde's name could hardly be acceptable, and Mrs. Tanqueray might also be thought embarrassing company and her tale possibly too long and too heavy. Balmoral's selected piece was *Liberty Hall* and that certainly could not be accused of intellectual profundity or feared because of ethical impropriety. It raises no question of conduct and it is as far as possible from attacking the higher ranges of the intellect.

Liberty Hall seemed to me, when I read it in 1954, as childish as it was harmless; doubtless it acted then, under Alexander's leadership, much better than it reads now. The plot is feuilleton stuff about the two daughters of Sir Norman Chilworth. These unfortunate young ladies, having had considerable financial hopes, find themselves with nothing at all. The entailed Chilworth estates have passed to a distant cousin and, this being the eighteen-nineties, the stranded daughters of a Knight (or baronet) could not possibly be expected to go out and earn a living unless it were of some very genteel description, such as the colouring of Christmas cards. (The daughter called Blanche did so far yield to commerce.) The Chilworth girls go, all forlorn, to stay with a Mr. Todman in Bloomsbury. He is a more or less bankrupt bookseller, but he had married " poor Mama's sister." So he is a once-embarrassing but now rather useful relation of the Chilworth blood. Todman's occupation of bookselling, though economically fatal, seemed at least more respectable in the eyes of Victorian gentlefolk than did most retail trade. His shabby home is the Liberty Hall of the play's title and the refuge of the young Misses Chilworth.

In the Bloomsbury back parlour the playwright, remembering " Caste," could raise laughs from the vulgar commoners who have haddocks as a relish to their tea. Hither, also, there meanders a curious stranger called Mr. Owen, a gentleman of uncertain means and occupation. Would you believe that he turns out to be the Distant Cousin and Heir to the Chilworth Estates? In the end this mystery man, whose mystery is obvious the moment he appears, emerges as a general benefactor. He rescues Todman from debt by his cheque-book, Blanche Chilworth from spinsterhood by his courtship, and he sees Amy Chilworth safely into the arms of the Hon. Gerald Harringay, a political aspirant " whose Governor wants him to be in the Lower House."

It is rash to laugh at plays out of period, rash to laugh at such speeches as have to be delivered. Mr. Owen, whose offer of a hand and flowers has been rejected by Blanche Chilworth, thus makes his farewell over his spurned bouquet:

> " Meanwhile I owe it to my own self-respect that the same roof shall not cover us for another night or for another hour. Time may yet undeceive you—I trust to Time. I leave behind me many foolish hopes that I once dared to cherish. Like my flowers—they are fading—at your feet."

After all, this farewell of a rejected lover has a ring of style, a certain rhythm in its diction, and some dignity as well as the pomposity which seems so curious and even absurd to us now. Noël Coward set a fashion for almost monosyllabic dialogue and the popular critics are now accustomed to denounce as " literary," as though that were some un-pardonable vice, any modern play in which the characters pass beyond the curt, the slangy, and the trivial in speech. But a change must come and future playgoers may regard with astonishment the stuff that passed for dramatic dialogue in the 1920s and after. We can write off R. C. Carton's plot as puerile, but we cannot safely dismiss the fuller speech and more open emotionalism employed by the St. James's Theatre Company in 1895. At any rate, *Liberty Hall* was chosen by the Queen for the command performance at Balmoral and it pleased.

My authority for this is Allan Aynesworth. At the age of ninety, and happily proving that the sea-coast of Bohemia can be a healthy nurse of longevity, he very kindly sent me his notes on the performance in which he appeared at the age of thirty-one.

The visit was arranged to take place during the Scottish section of Alexander's autumn tour of 1895. The company left Glasgow by special train on Sunday morning and arrived at Ballater in the evening. They slept in a hotel at Ballater and were driven up to Balmoral on the following afternoon. They were made comfortable, saw the lay-out of the stage, and dressed and made-up. The performance did not start until about nine-thirty. At the close they were presented, each in turn, in a room bedecked in tartan. After that they were served with a most sumptuous hot dinner.

The Queen sat in the front row with a small table in front of her. On this stood her handkerchiefs and a little bell which she tinkled when she was ready for the curtain to rise on each act, after discovering, presumably, that the players were ready too, since there is a change of scene in *Liberty Hall*.

The audience included Prince Louis of Battenberg, husband of the Queen's granddaughter. Allan Aynesworth describes him as " looking splendid in full Highland evening dress." (Something there to enrage the anti-Balmoralists.) There were also a number of guests from shooting parties and workers on the estate. The Queen, he writes, thoroughly enjoyed the comedy scenes, and at times had her handkerchief to her eyes; this must have been when the sufferings of the Chilworths and the rejection of Mr. Owen by Blanche were to the fore. Those who remember the more than elegant Alexander can well imagine with what handsome grace he bade farewell to " the many hopes I once dared to cherish. Like my flowers—they are fading—at your feet." We can visualise the curtain falling on these lines. Surely this was the moment when " something like moisture conglobed " in the royal eyes.

The programme ran as follows:

BALMORAL CASTLE

MONDAY, 16TH SEPTEMBER, 1895

An original comedy in Four Acts
by
R. C. CARTON
entitled

LIBERTY HALL

MR. OWEN	*Mr. George Alexander*
WILLIAM TODMAN	*Mr. E. M. Robson*
HON. GERALD HARRINGAY	*Mr. Allan Aynesworth*

MR. PEDRICK (Solicitor)	*Mr. Arthur Royston*
J. BRIGINSHAW	*Mr. H. H. Vincent*
ROBERT BINKS (Todman's Shop Boy)	*Master Jones*
LUSCOMBE	*Mr. Frank Dyall*
MR. HICKSON } Brother and Sister {	*Mr. F. Kinsey Peile*
MISS HICKSON }	*Miss Winifred Dolan*
CRAFER (Todman's Servant)	*Miss M. Mouillot*
AMY CHILWORTH { Daughters of the late Sir Norman Chilworth	*Miss Furtado Clarke*
BLANCHE CHILWORTH	*Miss Evelyn Millard*

ACT 1   CHILWORTH (*four months elapse*)

ACT 2   BACK PARLOUR OF MR. TODMAN'S SHOP,
               CHEEPE STREET, BLOOMSBURY, W.C.

ACT 3   THE SAME (*a month later*)

ACT 4   THE SAME (*early next morning*)

The Scenery by H. P. Hall and Stanley Hoban

STAGE DIRECTOR	*Mr. George Alexander*
ASSISTANT STAGE DIRECTOR	*Mr. H. H. Vincent*
SECRETARY	*Mr. Robert V. Shone*

It is noticeable that Alexander gave the title of Stage Director to what was later called Producer and is now being once more called Director, since that is the prevailing American usage. Frank Dyall, who had a small man-servant's part, was later to become famous as Franklin Dyall, excellent in all strong or sinister parts, in which his depth of voice was a great asset. Evelyn Millard became the reigning beauty of the Theatre in Edwardian London. She played a succession of damsels in distress in Lewis Waller's cloak-and-sword dramas; these plays would now be dismissed as romantic flap-doodle and would not be endured without music. Ivor Novello discovered that by the addition of acceptable tunes romance can still be the box-office champion of a supposedly hard-boiled generation. In *Liberty Hall* Evelyn Millard's Blanche must have been a cause of tears no less decorative than was George Alexander in touching those heart-strings which the cautious Simon Tappertit said ought not to be " wibrated."

By the time the laughter and the " wibration," the presentations and the dining, were over, it was well into Tuesday morning. It was pouring in torrents when the carriages came round to take the company away down past Abergeldie to Ballater. The carriages were not supposed to drive up to the Royal Entrance of the Castle, but the Queen specially sent down an equerry to insist that this entrance (or rather exit) should be used by the players since departure by the usual door would mean a walk to the vehicles through the downpour and a long drive with wet clothes and feet. This act of thoughtfulness at so late an hour was much appreciated by the potential victims of the cataract.

So the horse-transport trotted off to Ballater and a short night's rest. The Company had five hours' sleep before getting into the special train which took them to Edinburgh. It had been a hard week-end, but much enjoyed. There the publicity of the Royal Command created a stampede to see the Queen's chosen play at the Lyceum Theatre on Tuesday night. The rest of the week yielded performances with packed houses. Among the oddities and excitements of the evening one little event stayed in Allan Aynesworth's memory. The call-boy was found giving a lecture on the art of acting to a bearded dignitary, who was in fact the Cabinet Minister in residence. The players were shocked at the boy's impertinence: the Minister thanked the child heartily for giving him some interesting information by which a politician might well profit.

Queen Victoria encouraged acting, especially the elocutionary side of acting, in her family. An actor called George Bartley was employed as their coach. The children were well grounded in languages and could be rhetorical in French and German as well as in English. There was some fun, and early fun, to mitigate this service of the Muses. The Prince of Wales was taken to Astley's Circus at the age of four; but at seven he was introduced to Shakespeare. That was absurd, a policy produced, no doubt, by the somewhat owlish Baron Stockmar whose intentions were all too lofty and who had high notions of leading the young idea to all things Great and Good. Stockmar's gravity had worked well enough with Prince Albert, a natural recipient of learning and edification. But it did not do so well with the Queen's eldest son, in whom there was something of the Old Adam ineradicable by the new pedant. Concerning Edward VII, Sir Sydney Lee[1] supposed—and no doubt rightly—that " a surfeit of Shakespeare in his early theatrical experiences accounts for a marked diminution of his enthusiasm for the national dramatist as his career came to a close. A pantomime or a farce proved from the first rather more attractive." However, there were some early escapes from boredom and the Bard. John Henry Anderson, " The Wizard of the North," was invited to Balmoral that he might display the conjurer's arts to the royal children. " Papa," said Master Bertie later, " knows how all these tricks are

[1] *Edward VII,* by Sir Sidney Lee. Vol. 1, p. 20.

done." There was no getting round that serious, sharp-eyed, informative parent. Stockmar, no doubt, was thinking that the boy would be better served by the compulsion to learn the part of Prospero than by enjoyment of a hired and contemporary magician.

The application of the young Princes and Princesses to the more exalted forms of theatre was steady and severe. The Prince of Wales's repertory, adds Sir Sidney Lee, included scenes from Racine's *Athalie* in which he took the part of Abner and his sister, the Princess Royal, that of Athalie, as well as dramatised extracts from Thomson's *The Seasons*, in which the Prince of Wales represented Winter with a white beard and a cloak with icicles—or what seemed to be such. On the thirteenth anniversary of their parents' wedding-day the royal children performed some of Schiller's *Wallenstein*. A future devotee of farce and pantomime was thus, quite naturally, in the making.

Later in life the Prince of Wales was a constant playgoer and close friend of the more eminent players in vaudeville as well as in " the legitimate." This friendship, as well as this patronage, did much to raise the social status of the English theatre and of its artists. On his fiftieth birthday five leaders of the profession, representing managers and actors, went down to Sandringham to make a presentation of a gold cigar-box in gratitude for the Prince's valuable support of the English theatre.

After becoming King, Edward VII invited the players frequently to Sandringham and to Windsor; there were thirty-two " Commands " during his reign and all the leading actors and actresses appeared at one or other castle in their successes of the year. The lighter stage was not forgotten. Dan Leno shared a bill with Seymour Hicks and Ellaline Terriss: Albert Chevalier sang his Cockney songs, Pélissier brought *The Follies* and Adeline Genée danced at some of these occasions. But there were no such invitations during the autumnal residences at Balmoral, which, after all, is a long way off.

In the following reign there was a return to Commands during the Highland holiday. Cyril Maude and his company were in Scotland in the autumn of 1913, before going to Canada, and they were requested to take a comedy by Wilfred Coleby called *The Headmaster* to entertain at Balmoral. After the war King George V and Queen Mary made a complete and very politic innovation by inviting unstarred companies to Deeside; this conferred the most valuable publicity and prestige on those who were in most need of such assistance. In one case the command was to a small and semi-amateur team which carried the proud title of the Scottish National Theatre Society. This pleasant compliment occurred in October in 1922, and the recognition of Scottish companies continued in the following reign. Both the Perth and the Dundee repertories have been invited, the former playing A. A. Milne's *The Fourth Wall* in 1938 and the latter C. K. Munro's *At Mrs. Beam's* in 1947.

A nice example of royal patronage for a small, but admirable, venture was the command given to the Travelling Theatre of the Arts League of Service in the autumn of 1925. The A.L.S.—to escape the somewhat dreary title of the League—had been founded in 1919 and its purpose was to bring all the arts into everyday life; one of many ideas and activities was the use of a touring caravan which would take an intelligent form of theatrical variety, songs and dances as well as short plays, to the towns and villages which rarely enjoyed anything but the mechanised entertainment of what are now called the " mass-media." When working for C.E.M.A. (Council for the Encouragement of Music and the Arts), later the Arts Council, I realised how much we had lost when the Travelling Theatre was given up, after eighteen years, in 1937. If a dozen such " theatres " with managements and artists only half as competent as were engaged in the A.L.S. had been available, they would have been most welcome all over the country and especially in the isolated areas where war industries were collecting large temporary populations with very few amenities or forms of recreation.

The Travelling Theatre, whose manager was Eleanor Elder, later assisted by Judith Wogan, involved very considerable hardships for its company. The work meant constant moving from one " fit-up " to another in village or town halls with the arrangement of stage and curtains and lighting. The possible receipts could not be large and the players, in addition to receiving inevitably small salaries, had to live off the land, like an invading army—but very much more popular. They were found hospitality and they made numerous friends; but to be a good, polite, conversational guest at the end of a long hard day can add to the labours. It was rare for them to perform anywhere without receiving a request to return.

At one time there were two separate companies at work in the South and North. Here were Strolling Players in the old vagabond tradition; but the Travelling Theatre none the less became a training school of considerable value and Bernard Shaw evoked an account of its life and adventures from Eleanor Elder by announcing that " all the people who are any good now have graduated in the A.L.S.," and by urging that its history should therefore be written. Shaw's " all " was going rather far, but a Thespian Wagon whose first journey had Angela and Hermione Baddeley as its juveniles was not starting in any inadequate manner. These sisters, who proceeded to careers equal in distinction though different in scope of work, were " on the road " in this hard way for the first two or three years of the A.L.S. The members of the two companies in 1925-26 included Rosalind Patrick (Iden), Donald Wolfit, Henry Cass, Mackenzie Ward, Leslie Mitchell, Cecil Landeau and a number of other names that were to become well known in various kinds of theatrical and radio work.

Scotland showed a great liking for the Travelling Theatre and one of its best loved artists was Hugh Mackay, a Gaelic speaker and singer from the Far North and a handyman, too, in many crafts. He became known as " Hebs " because his principle function was the solo singing of Hebridean songs which he rendered with both a spirited humour and a charming tenderness. He could take a share, too, in plays and concerted items and was practical in all affairs. The beauty of his singing in Gaelic must have greatly helped in winning the approval of Scottish audiences and of Scottish hostesses. Some of the latter were people of influence. The company was entertained by the Earl and Countess of Aberdeen at the House of Cromar and the Countess of Strathmore had taken some of them to Glamis after a very successful performance in Forfar. This brought a recommendation to the King and Queen and an invitation to Balmoral.

Here was a very different arrival from that of the West End stars with special trains. The players drove over from the House of Cromar: they were warned to give a light programme and it consisted to a great extent of the folk-songs, part-songs, and " absurdities " in which the Travelling Theatre specialised. Hugh Mackay had two appearances in *Songs of the Hebrides*, and the single play performed was *The Grand Cham's Diamond* by Alan Monkhouse.

Eleanor Elder records that the applause, which had to be led by the King and Queen, was ample and generous, that the miming of A. A. Milne's *The King's Breakfast* was much liked, and so was an absurdity called *Daisy Bell*.

The programme had to be very strictly timed and to finish by ten-thirty—much earlier than in Queen Victoria's days. Scarcely was the curtain down than the company was sent for. Eleanor Elder in her book *The Travelling Players* describes the presentation thus:

" The King and Queen spoke to all of us in turn. Queen Mary was very like her portraits, tall, stately, and resplendent with jewellery. She had a brilliant smile that came and went suddenly, and a very beautiful voice. She had enjoyed our performance, both the music and the dances; she had never heard songs in Gaelic before; she had liked our play, and could so well understand my part of the mother of the family who longed for something exciting to happen at least once in her life; did we really get hospitality wherever we went? Questions came with a little pause between each, and a steady scrutiny. Then she passed along the line and King George took her place. He had been chatting to ' Hebs ' and laughing heartily. Hebs explained what it was about. The King had asked: ' Was it true we had to dress in a pigsty once? ' And I told him, ' Yes, but that they were pedigree pigs.'

" There was a charming informality about the King; he

was very easy to talk to. Turning to Princess Victoria, who was standing in the background, he said: ' My sister saw you in London,' and brought her into the conversation. The little Duchess of York did not wait for any introduction, but came forward eagerly to speak to us all. We were dismissed with a kindly handshake from King George, who said: ' These people must be very tired. Will you see that they have supper and are well looked after? ' We bowed our way out. Our audience was over. The theatre had to be dismantled and packed, and we had eighteen miles to drive before we reached Tarland.

" It was 2 a.m. when we arrived at the House of Cromar."

Nowadays the royal family attend the theatre so frequently as usual playgoers that the Command Performance or *Performance in the Presence of Their Majesties*—a title subsequently preferred—has ceased to be an institution. It is common knowledge that, if music is required in the home, Princess Margaret can brilliantly provide it. Amateur theatricals and charades have often been included in the life at Balmoral. In Victorian times there was a vogue for " tableaux " which some of the guests found over-long, and the Suite were often called on to perform in these as well as in actual plays. The tradition of Drama in the Home established by Queen Victoria and Prince Albert has not been abandoned, but it has been sensibly modified. One hardly expects the youngest talent of the family to be applied now to Racine's *Athalie* and Schiller's *Wallenstein*. Prince Charles and Princess Anne will surely not be directed to find Solace and Pleasure, in the Jacobean phrase, on cultural heights as lofty and as craggy as are, geographically, the Cairngorm summits at their gates.

The Perth Repertory Theatre was invited to Balmoral

in October of 1938. This was the first invitation given by
King George VI and Queen Elizabeth. The latter would
have a natural interest in this company since her family
home, Glamis Castle, is no great distance from Perth. The
request was the more generous since the Perth " Rep.," now
well established, was then quite a young venture, and could
not call upon players with big " names." It has owed a great
deal to the energies of David Steuart and Marjorie Dence as
directors of the artistic and business sides respectively. In
the following summer, with this showing of royal favour for
encouragement, Perth courageously followed Malvern in
attempting a July Theatre Festival. There was a new play
by James Bridie, *The Golden Legend of Shults*, and Alec
Guinness, then known to the discriminating few rather than
to the millions who are now his devotees, took the part
of Shakespeare's Romeo with Pamela Stanley as his
Juliet. This has some relevance to the Balmoral theme since
Miss Stanley, two years earlier, had been most successful
in London as Queen Victoria in the Laurence Housman
play-sequence *Victoria Regina*. One of the episodes of this
is set at Balmoral with John Brown and Disraeli appearing.

It was intimated to the Perth players that the facilities for
theatrical production in the Balmoral Ballroom were limited.
A small stage was erected between twin staircases. The play
selected must have only one set and that set was not to
require more than one entrance and one window. (Of little
use that to French farces with their six-doored bachelor's
flats and a pretty lady behind, or emerging from, each one
of them!) A list of half a dozen possibles was sent up and
the choice fell on *The Fourth Wall* by A. A. Milne, a Haymarket success of 1928. Milne, incidentally, was one of the
authors whose contribution to the Travelling Theatre

programme had been much enjoyed by the parents of the present host and hostess. The cast was as follows:

THE FOURTH WALL

A DETECTIVE STORY IN THREE ACTS
BY A. A. MILNE

The play directed by WILLARD STOKER

JIMMY LUDGROVE	*Ninian Brodie*
SUSAN CUNNINGHAM	*Lorna Tarbat*
ADAMS	*Ronald Trounce*
EDWARD LAVERICK	*Malcolm Hayes*
EDWARD CARTER	*David Steuart*
MAJOR FOTHERGILL	*R. Eric Lee*
MRS. FULVERTON-FANE	*Marjorie Dence*
JANE WEST	*Helena Siddons*
ARTHUR LUDGROVE	*Willard Stoker*
P. C. MALLET	*Graham Anderson*
" SERGEANT " MALLET	*Patrick Kinsella*

The record in this case was much the same, except that the company stayed in Balmoral, using widely dispersed bedrooms, some a little hard to discover in the dead vast and middle of the night. The memories are of tartan and Landseer engravings. The smallness of the Ballroom, with the King and Queen so adjacent to the stage in their front-row seats, made for nervousness. But the enthusiastic reception soon eased that and the players did not feel the occasion as awesome. The atmosphere was that of a Country House party; the audience, with guests and servants, numbered about 300 at a guess.

Mr. Steuart records the same gracious and personal

entertainment with individual presentations of all the visitors. Before retiring the King and Queen came and said good night personally to each and thanked them again. " I was quite spellbound by the beauty of the Queen," David Steuart has written to me, " since now I realised that photographs did no justice to it at all. That night she was in a black crinoline dress with tiara and was a perfect picture."

The Dundee Repertory Theatre was similarly invited in September, 1947. Another local recognition was thus given and another of the neighbours of Glamis honoured. Here again the company was one of those hard-slogging " Reps." which make the stars of to-morrow instead of employing the stars of to-day. The play this time was C. K. Munro's *At Mrs. Beam's*, originally a Stage Society Sunday night production, but later a very popular comedy in which a Scottish actress, Jean Cadell, had once given a delightful performance as the boarding-house spinster, Miss Shoe.

The production was by A. R. Whatmore, who served Dundee long and well. The cast was as follows:

MISS SHOE	*Sara Payne*
MR. DURROWS	*Newton Blick*
MISS CHEEZLE	*Gertrude Sterroll*
MRS. BEBB	*Ethel Ramsay*
JAMES BEBB	*Richard Todd*
MRS. STONE	*Yvonne Hills*
MISS NEWMAN	*Sheila Gibbs*
MRS. BEAM	*Nora Gordon*
MR. DERMOTT	*Michael Rose*
LAURA PASQUALE	*Nancy Mansfield*
COLIN	*Joseph Greig*

Alec Robertson, then a director of the theatre, has given me some of his memories. In addition to a full gathering of the Royal Family, with guests, tenants, and staff, Queen Juliana of the Netherlands was present. The interval music was provided by gramophone discs selected by Princess Margaret: it was of the " ultra-modern type."

The recollections resemble those of the Perth Company, a most receptive audience and wonderful hospitality. The Queen's charm and friendliness were conspicuous. There were moments of fright; especially nervous was the electrician who feared that he might fuse the lights of the whole Castle since he had taken all his leads off a single plug point. But there was no need for the King to cry for torches as did Hamlet's uncle during another and imaginary Command Performance. The supper was superb, but one rigid vegetarian member of the team, confronted with venison, grouse and salmon, was asking timidly whether she could have an egg. The company left at four in the morning and drove back by the mountain road over the Devil's Elbow to Glen Shee. It is a nasty drive without preceding festivity. But the driver got them home without accident.

Incidentally, an earlier Dundonian, the busker-poet McGonagall, had called at Balmoral in Victorian times with a view to reciting Shakespeare's works and his own. Unfortunately the gate-keepers were not co-operative. He got no further. Doubtless McGonagall did look a trifle queer. But if the Queen had been in the right mood, she might have liked the man and his Muse too. For he was a most loyal poet and had praised the adjacent river with a nonpareil among non-sequiturs:

" The hen it is a bonny bird
And so's the River Dee."

and in his great Ode on the New Tay Bridge, he exclaimed:

" And as you have been opened on the 20th day of June,
I hope Her Majesty Queen Victoria will visit thee very soon;
Because thou art worthy of a visit from Duke, Lord or Queen,
And strongly and securely built, which is most worthy to be
seen—
Near by Dundee and the bonnie Magdalen Green."

The Queen was to cross it, securely, many a time.

It was not in the order of things that the New Drama of the theatrical progressives should be imported to any of the old castles. Queen Victoria paid her compliments to the St. James's Theatre company by her command of *Liberty Hall*, and that was a salute to the elegance of presentation and to the well-mannered performance of a distinguished company, for leading which George Alexander was then renowned. King Edward VII had been surfeited with the classics in his childhood. His favourite kind of theatre was that of Hawtrey's smiling mischief in a comedy from the French, a theatre of stylish levity and of civilised trifling.

King George V and Queen Mary, alive to the changing climate of taste and opinion, made an original and valuable recognition of the young players roughing it on the roughest roads and their successors, no less alive to new movements, encouraged the Scottish Repertories which sprang up during the nineteen-thirties and have held on courageously and none too easily in the present years of rising costs and TV competition.

So Balmorality, as far as it has touched and influenced the

theatre, has given its stamp of helpful approval to things judged good in their time, whether they were products of West-End *expertise* or of the workaday " Reps." which struggle, amid so many difficulties, to make the drama a national, as well as a metropolitan, institution.

CHAPTER TEN

Visitors' Book

THE visitors who have been given bed and board at
Balmoral have ranged from a Tsar of All the Russias
to small-part actors: artists and ecclesiastics have been
fellow guests. Nearly all British Cabinet Ministers of note
have taken their turns of official residence. So it has
happened that decisions not only of national but of world-
wide importance have been made beside the waters of the
Dee. Now that communications by telephone, wireless and
air have destroyed the handicap of distance in maintaining
social and political relations, there is no necessity for the
Sovereign to have a Minister always by his or her side;
there is the Private Secretary staying at the house called
Craigowan within the Castle grounds and he goes across
daily to his work. But Ministers do still come up on special
occasions.

One of the earliest visitors after the discovery of Deeside
and the occupation of Balmoral II was the diarist Greville,
not a writer to whom the reader would look for much
sympathy or sugary comment. In September of 1849 he
took the long drive over from Perth by way of the Spital of
Glenshee and found his stay, though brief, delightful. There
was not a sign of sourness or mischief in what he wrote.

"Much as I dislike Courts and all that appertains to them, I am glad to have made this expedition and to have seen the Queen and Prince in this Highland retreat where they certainly appear to great advantage. The place is very pretty and the house very small. They live there without any state whatever; they live not merely like private gentle-folks, but like very small gentle-folks, small house, small rooms, small establishment. There are no soldiers and the whole guard of the Sovereign and of the whole Royal Family is a single policeman who walks about the grounds to keep off impertinent intruders or improper characters . . . they live with the greatest simplicity and ease. The Prince shoots every morning, returns to luncheon, and then they walk or drive. The Queen is running in and out of the house all day long; often goes about alone, and walks into cottages, sits down, and chats with the old women." This is fair and genial comment from one always ready to be critical: Greville was genuinely surprised by the happiness discovered on Deeside where the formalities of London and Windsor life could be forgotten.

The visitor accompanied the Royal Family to the Gathering and Games at Braemar, still a simple outing to a simply conducted local occasion. "A pretty sight enough" he found it to be. After dinner the company went to the only sitting-room that there was in addition to the dining-room. It served for drawing-room, billiard-room and library. The Queen, Prince, and her ladies went back to the dining-room where the table was pushed aside and they were given lessons in dancing the reel. Greville and Lord John Russell were not admitted to this exercise: so they played billiards.

Sir Edwin Landseer paid his first visit in the following year. He had been born in a period notable for its Infant

Phenomena. When he was a child Master Betty, the Young Roscius, was triumphantly berattling the English stage, which he had first captured when a boy of eleven. Unlike Master Betty, Landseer did not find himself too old at seventeen, the age at which the acting prodigy became a target for derision. Betty, whose real name was West, was " goosed," in the language of the time, for his performance of Richard III. After that he lived in obscurity to the age of eighty-three.

Much happier was Landseer's march down the years. The start was not so fantastically swift and the House of Commons was never asked to adjourn to see one of his canvases, as it was to see Master Betty as Hamlet in 1805. But the young Edwin exhibited at the Royal Academy at thirteen, and was made A.R.A. at the earliest permitted age, twenty-four. He was soon in royal favour and painted his first portrait of the Queen before her marriage and frequently drew or painted her family; at Balmoral and in London he gave lessons in drawing to the Queen and her children. Both Victoria and the Princess Royal, Vicky, were apt pupils.

He was knighted in the year of his first stay, 1850. In 1851 he painted *The Monarch of the Glen* for the House of Lords, but the House of Commons refused to pay for it. This blend of romance and realism in painting has long ceased to please critical taste, but pictures of this kind were deemed the perfect ornament of Stag Party castle walls for many years to come and *The Monarch* still fetched a price of £7,000 in 1892. The Queen had seen work of his at Ardverikie before she came to Balmoral and was to see it again at Glen Feshie during one of the Great Expeditions. She recorded the incident thus: " We got off our ponies and went into one of the huts to look at a fresco of stags of

Landseer's over a chimney-piece." Landseer was a fast and prolific draughtsman and painter and was apt to leave his mark wherever he stayed. The walls in the Lodge at the east end of Loch Affric are covered with his murals as well as with engravings of his larger work. Balmoral is rich in Landseers and has some of his best work. It is customary to smile, or even jeer, at his name now, but his draughtsman-ship was masterly as can be seen, not only in his portraits of the eminent, but in the drawings of deer and his heads of the Balmoral ghillies. A complete volume of all Landseer's engravings was photographed and set in a bound volume for the Queen after his death in 1873.

In 1855 " Fritz of Prussia," who had been taking the baths at Ostend, came, as it was said, to inspect Scotland, and his journey included Balmoral. In fact Prince Frederick had in mind the courtship of Princess Victoria and the achievement of the match which had long been in the mind of his elders. Von Moltke, whose ideas of strategy were not limited to war, followed the Prince as companion and adviser. He was at once struck with the fact that the Royal Family behaved, at least at Balmoral, in an easy and familiar manner. He commented, in his correspondence, on the unpretentious way of life without guards or a host of flunkeys. To him it was astounding that the Court of one of the most powerful States was in residence in such a spot and that from these remote mountains the fate of the world might be determined. He approved the engagement that followed from the walk in Glen Girnoch: much British opinion, voiced especially by *The Times*, did not.

Gladstone was Minister in residence at the end of August, 1863. He related that he immediately took a walk of 24¾ miles—how careful the measurement! It was no small

outing for a man of fifty-three; naturally he suffered from
stiffness afterwards and complained that his day of " long
stretches " had gone by. But he was not to be held down.
After a fine hill scramble of over three hours he lamented
that with light and opportunity he would have been ready
for another. On the following day he did a nineteen-mile
walk up Lochnagar and came back " fresh as a lark." The
Queen had warned him not to attempt the summit in mist
and rain—" Mist there was with rain to boot," he wrote.
" I find the resemblance to Snowdon rather striking. It is
3,800 feet: we went up to about 3,300 feet." The night
before that he had been to the ghillies' ball at Abergeldie.
The Queen, of course in mourning, stayed at Balmoral
feeling " very low, on account of the ball which, of course,
recalled so much." " The Princes danced with great
activity after deer-stalking and very well. There was a dance
called the perpetual jig, nearly the best fun I ever witnessed."
The secret of perpetual motion seems almost to have been
solved in the keen air of Deeside, with the young Prince of
Wales as host.

Gladstone has left an account of Victoria's range of conversation. " I dined with the Queen again last night; also
Lady Augusta Bruce—seven, again, in all. The Crown
Princess had a headache, as well she might, so they were not
there. The same royalties as before, and everything quite as
pleasing. The Queen talked Shakespeare, Scott, the use of
the German language in England (and there I could not
speak out *all* my mind), Guizot's translation of the Prince's
speeches, and his preface (which the Queen has since sent
me to look at), the children's play at Windsor (when Princess
Alice acted a high priest, with great success—in *Athalie*, I
think), handwritings, Lord Palmerston's to wit, Mr.

Disraeli's style in his letters to the Queen, the proper mode of writing, on what paper, etc., and *great* laudation of Lady Lyttelton's letters. Princess Alice declares her baby is pretty, and says she shall show it me. The Queen was very cheerful, and seemed for the time happy. A statue of the Prince is about to be set up at Aberdeen, and she is then to attend and receive an address, with Sir G. Grey present in due form. The household life is really very agreeable when one comes to know them. One way and another they have a great deal in them."

The Minister obliged his hostess by translating into verse a passage from Schiller's *Wallenstein*, which deeply touched her continuing mood of desolation.

> " *Too well I know the treasure I have lost.*
> *From off my life the bloom is swept away;*
> *It lies before me cold and colourless;*
> *For he, that stood beside me like my youth,*
> *He charmed reality into a dream,*
> *And over all the common face of things*
> *He shed the golden glow of morning's blush;*
> *And in the fire of his affection*
> *Dull forms, that throng the life of every day,*
> *Yea to mine own amazement, tow'red aloft.*
> *Win what I may henceforth, the Beautiful*
> *Is gone, and gone without return.*"

The Gladstonian walks went on, sixteen miles, twenty-five miles with " a measured mile in twelve minutes beside this beautiful Dee." On another night the Queen was in full spate of conversation.

" I can hardly tell you all the things talked about—

Prince Humbert, Garibaldi, Lady Lyttelton, the Hagley boys, Lucy, smoking, dress, fashion, Prince Alfred, his establishment and future plans, Prince of Wales's visit to Denmark, revenue, Lancashire, foreign policy, the newspaper press, the habits of the present generation, young men, young married ladies, clubs, Clarendon's journey, the Prince Consort on dress and fashion, Prince of Wales on ditto, Sir R. Peel, F. Pell, Mrs. Stonor, the rest of that family, misreading foreign names and words, repute of English people abroad, happy absence of foreign office disputes and quarrels."

Gladstone was there when the Queen's carriage, coming back from Loch Muick, was first taken up a wrong and rough track and then overturned. He advised her to give up these drives in the dark. But she replied that she felt the hours that came before dinner wearisome without them. The " Three Prussian Children " arrived, her grandchildren by Vicky and Prince Frederick. " The Queen says the baby is not pretty—the little boy on coming yesterday called them all stumpfnase, pug-nosed." Presumably this was the child who was to be Kaiser William II. It sounds like him. Gladstone recounted that the little black boy, Willem, who waited on Princess Alice, amazed Deeside and that one of the local laundry-women said nothing would induce her to wash his clothes as the black would certainly come off. Gladstone wrote much genial gossip to his wife and decided that " The people, one and all, are very easy to get on with and Windsor, I suppose, stiffens them a little." Unfortunately, the future relations of Gladstone and the Queen were not to be so happy.

The Queen was devoted to animals, especially to her dogs

and to the Balmoral ponies. In 1869 these ponies caused, if not a storm in a teacup, what turned out to be a long-drawn rumpus in a stable. Three visitors were the cause of trouble. These were Canon Duckworth, with whom the Queen discussed the future of the Prince of Wales, Edgar Boehm, a sculptor often employed by the Queen, and Hermann Sahl, the German Secretary whose main task was that of arranging and preserving correspondence and drafting suitable messages to foreign sovereigns when they were in mourning or expecting a congratulation. These three preferred riding to the gigantic walks which the more strenuous Gladstone so much enjoyed. Between them they involved Colonel Ponsonby, the Equerry in Waiting, and later Private Secretary, in a tiresome and ridiculous row. The story has been told at some length in Sir Frederick Ponsonby's *Sidelights on Queen Victoria*, and it is worth summarising in brief.

The Balmoral ponies were sturdy and docile. They demanded no skill of horsemanship and so the rider could set out for the hills in confidence. His chief business was to sit still. Sir Henry observed of the fractious visitors that not one of them would have dared to mount a full-sized or spirited horse. But the ponies could be, and were, much coveted by them. As a result, the poor beasts were overworked by their inexpert mounts, who seemed to imagine they were using mechanical transport. They urged their animals up steep hills as though they were indefatigable and nervously tugged at the reins on difficult ground. The visitors had a habit of ordering ponies as a matter of right and when the Queen discovered that the right was abused and the ponies distressed and damaged by ignorant and inexpert riders, she determined to stop it. She did not, however, issue a personal fiat. She left the matter to Colonel Ponsonby and he had to do something about it. His insistence that the ponies were not a " free for all " perquisite of guests started a ludicrous set of quarrels. Apparently he was not allowed to state definitely that the Queen was giving a direct command; he could only suggest that he gave no order without it being desired.

When the three guilty parties saw their ponies denied them, while grooms smiled and sniffed, and other visitors and even servants were still riding out, they flamed up. Artists are often difficult and Boehm was furious. The Canon apparently felt that the dignity of the Church was impugned. Sahl had an inferiority complex because he was at Balmoral as a German civilian and German civilians were despised by Germans with military titles. Ponsonby was a Colonel and so he must, in Sahl's eye, be acting " with military exclusiveness and jealousy towards non-officers in the Army." He even sent a furious letter to the Queen about the arrogance and insolence of the domineering soldier. This fantastic dispute was carried on by lengthy letter-writing from one member of the House Party to another and transmitted from room to room by footmen for over two months. Having fired off their epistles the combatants would then have to meet at meals in the Castle and pretend that there was no tension of any kind.

Laurence Housman brings this comedy of " Stable Government " into his sequence of short plays in *The Golden Sovereign* and introduces John Brown to the tangle as a counsellor of common-sense and manipulator of peace. Brown tells the Queen that he has a " poor opinion of Mr. Bum, who, if he even took riding-lessons at all, took 'em from watching Canon Duckworth, which is the catchingness

of ignorance, as I've told ye." Sir Henry Ponsonby leaves
John Brown out of it, and concludes:

" Queen Victoria, who undoubtedly was kept fully
informed by Lady Churchill of all that had passed, must
have been very much amused at this storm in a tea-cup,
but she had saved her dear hill ponies from any possible
harm, and that, to her, was far more important than the
wounded feelings of her guests."

In the play the Queen gives tactful advice to the combatants
on the merits of walking exercise. It is a pity that Mr.
Gladstone was not there at the time. He could have led
Secretary Stahl, Mr. Bum, and the peevish Canon on his
unwearying way. Twenty-five miles, perhaps, and that
measured mile in twelve minutes. That would have " larned
them to be toads " to ponies.

While Prince Albert was alive the Queen and he always
took dinner with the suite and the Minister-in-Residence.
The latter sat on the Queen's left and the Prince on her
right. Mrs. Lindsay recounts a singular piece of rudeness
on the part of Lord Palmerston when he was at Balmoral.
" Pam " was in a temper about something and deliberately
omitted to take the usual place of honour; instead he took
the seat allotted to her father, Dr. Robertson, the Commissioner, and so left that poor man with no place except
that next the Queen, which he could not occupy without a
special command. " After a very uncomfortable minute or
two," Mrs. Lindsay wrote, " the lady-in-waiting—Lady
Churchill I think it was—observed his position and with
kind and ready tact moved next to the Queen herself and
motioned my father to take her place. Lord Palmerston

calmly ate his dinner without explanation or apology."
After the Queen went into mourning she dined in the
Library with members of the family; the guests and
members of the suite were invited on occasion and a few
at a time to join them. The Minister, if not thus bidden,
dined alone in his own room, which was not com-
modious. If Lord Palmerston had been at Balmoral then
he might have had many lonely evenings.

In those years smoking was regarded as an exceptional
exercise, and accepted as such by men as well as by women.
Even in Clubs men retired to a special smoking-room and
the rest of the premises were kept uncontaminated; that
rule held for a long time at the Athenæum. Out and about
the smoker could enter a cigar-divan and recline for his
indulgence. In the home it was common to wear a special
uniform of smoking-cap and smoking-jacket so that the
detested fumes would not be carried into general company.
The idea of smoking immediately after, or even through, a
meal would have been deemed altogether outrageous.

The Queen detested the habit and, although she allowed
a smoking-room at Balmoral, she imposed a timetable and a
discipline upon both her visitors and her family. In 1869
she sent a note to Lord Charles Fitzroy, who was acting as
Master of the Household, commanding him to see that the
den conceded to masculine weakness was always closed at
midnight. She laid it down that late sessions with tobacco
were " a thing which in her house the Queen does not
intend to allow." They were bad, she said, for the guests
and set a bad example to the servants. Lord Charles was
ordered " quietly and effectively " to remind the Princes
and the gentlemen that the hour had struck and there was
to be no more nicotine. It must have embarrassed the Master

of the Household to be thus forced to interrupt a jovial sitting and to anticipate the modern public-house cry of " Time, Gentlemen, please." But this was a subject on which the Queen was at her firmest. Hence this curfew for cigars, but, in view of active sporting operations in the morning, a reasonably late one.

Gladstone was back again in 1871. That was the year when he dined at Abergeldie with the Prince of Wales whom he found " far lighter in hand than the Duke of Edinburgh." (The Duke was the Prince's younger brother and the Queen's second son.) How light in hand the Prince found Gladstone is a matter for surmise but the two seem to have got on surprisingly well together. They played cards and the Prince displayed a remarkable skill. There was an unsuccessful effort made to get Gladstone deer-stalking; the latter excused himself on the grounds of eyesight, but physically he was up to anything.

Now at the age of sixty-seven he continued his vigorous and lengthy tramps, with a keen eye on his watch and his time-schedules. On 4th September of that year he recorded in his diary a walk of fifteen miles in four hours and five minutes, on 6th September twenty miles in five hours and forty-five minutes, and on 7th September another fifteen miles, time unstated. The tramps were presumably taken, at least in part, over the country, which is mainly rough, and not just along the Ballater and Braemar roads. He found great exaltation of mind and spirits, as well as delightful exercise, on the hills around Balmoral. Nothing, he wrote, set him up more, nothing more conduced to intellectual energy.

It was very different with Disraeli, who made two visits to the Castle and was never in Gladstonian fettle there. In the end the Queen excused him on grounds of ill-health from further attendance in Deeside. In September, 1868, he went by train to Perth and was so well equipped in the matter of hampers that he wrote to his wife: " You provided for me so admirably and judiciously that I had two sumptuous meals; a partridge breakfast and a chicken and tongue dinner with plenty of good wine." It was the custom then to drive from Perth or Dunkeld over the Spital of Glenshee and the Devil's Elbow, a long journey involving a severe climb of over 2,000 feet and therefore a slow journey too. Disraeli did not reach the Castle until half-past nine at night, when the household was at dinner. The Queen sent a considerate message that he need not dress, but he preferred to dine in his room and to present himself at breakfast on the next morning. He was told by Lord Bridport not to wear a frock-coat. That evening he dined in the Library, " a small, square room, very cosy—like dining with a bachelor in very good rooms in the Albany." The company was " the Queen, Prince and Princess Christian, Princess Louise, the Duke of Edinburgh, and myself with Lord Bridport and Lady Churchill. Conversation lively, though not memorable. The Duke of Edinburgh talked much of foreign fruits and talked well."

The " plenty of good wine " consumed on the train journey had been sherry, which was injudicious. " Although my diet has been severe I have not tasted anything but sherry since we parted," he told his wife, " and I have suffered much from biliary derangement which weakens and depresses me." A week later his health was very unsatisfactory and he again stated that he had drunk nothing but sherry, which strikes one as preposterous folly. It is small wonder that he complained of being in " a miserable state in the morning hours when I have to do the main work and the work is very heavy." If the Deeside climate did not suit Disraeli, he certainly encouraged it to be vexatious. It has been well said of travel that it may harden the liver as well as broaden the mind and Disraeli's habits were unkind to a man of a bilious disposition. The weather at first was wet and warm and his room too hot: he combated this by opening the window, which he seems to have regarded as an adventurous thing to do. He then let the fire nearly out and got the temperature to his liking.

He was able to walk in the grounds—no twenty-mile tramps for him—and despite " the biliary derangement " he found the views admirable. Not only were the mountains " of graceful outline," but the gardens reminded him of home. " An expanse of green and shaven lawn more extensive than that from the terrace of Clifden, and singularly striking in a land of mountains; but H.M. told me, that it was all artificial, and they had levelled a rugged and undulating soil. In short, our garden at Hughenden on a great scale: except this was a broad, green glade, the flower garden being at the other side of the Castle. I dined with the household, and, between ourselves, was struck, as I have been before, by the contrast between the Queen's somewhat simple, but sufficient, dinner, and the banquet of our humbler friends."

Next day he was taken for a drive to some famous water-falls and though the day was misty, he could write enthusiastically to Mrs. Disraeli that he never saw anything more magnificent. Switzerland had grander falls, but " none with such lovely accessories, such banks of birchen woods and boulders of colossal granite." On the following morning there was " one of those expeditions you read of in the

Queen's books, two carriages posting and changing horses.
We went to the Castle of Braemar where, every year, the
contiguous clans assemble. The castle is very picturesque
and is complete and inhabited and in old days must have
been formidable, as it commands all the passes of the valleys.
I was glad there were no Games." They drove on to the
Linn of Dee and had a well-approved picnic: " One might
take many hints for country luncheons from this day, for
our friends have great experience in these matters: and
nothing could be more compact and complete than the whole
arrangements. The party was very merry: all the courtiers
had a holiday. Lady Churchill said that, when she asked the
Queen, through the Princess Louise, whether she was
wanted this morning, the Queen replied, ' All the ladies
are to go, to make it amusing to Mr. Disraeli.' "

On the way they took tea with Lady Fife at Mar Lodge.
There was another lady there to entertain the Prime
Minister. " There we found Sylvia Doyle, looking more
absurd than any human being I can well remember. The
Highlanders call her ' The coloured Lady.' Her cheeks
were like a clown's in a pantomime, and she had a pile of
golden hair as high as some of the neighbouring hills.
However, she smiled and cracked her jokes as usual, and
gave me, as usual, a long list of all the places she was going
to." The final sentence suggests that Disraeli was not
altogether amused. His health was not improved by this
outing. He complained of extreme nervousness and the
continued consumption of sherry did not help. He left with
gifts from the Queen, two volumes of views of Balmoral, a
box full of family photographs, a whole length portrait of the
Prince, and " a Scotch shawl for Mrs. Disraeli, which H.M.
hopes you will find warm in the cold weather." The luggage

of the parting guest must have been bulky. But all these compliments and generosities did not relieve his pains. Before he finally left he resolved to stay in his room, " greatly suffering."

It had not been a success. He was continually coping with numerous and important dispatches as well as with his liver. He wrote sadly to Bishop Wilberforce, " Carrying on the Government of a Country six hundred miles from the metropolis doubles the labour." Others were to think the same.

Six years later the many miles were covered once more; and once more there was ill health. He had again made the long drive over the Devil's Elbow. " I have not been well here," he wrote to Lady Bradford, " and had it not been for Sir William Jenner might have been very ill. All is ascribed to my posting in an open carriage from Dunkeld to Balmoral, but the day was delicious and I was warmly clothed and never apprehended danger. I felt queer on Wednesday, though I dined with the Queen. On Thursday, Sir William kept me to my room and I have not left the Castle since."

The personal relations with the Queen were now of the most cordial kind. She was the Faery and " more than kind: she opens her heart to me on all subjects and shows me the most secret and most interesting correspondence." When the Duke of Edinburgh asked the Queen at dinner whether she had read *Lothair* she answered that she was the first person who read it. " The Duchess then rashly asked her Gracious Majesty whether she did not think Theodore a divine character: the Queen looked a little perplexed and grave." Perhaps she had been thinking of another work of the same name! However, " free from all shyness, she spoke

219

with great animation and happy expression, opening all her heart and mind to me."

Sir William Jenner insisted on putting a mustard plaster on Disraeli's back and the good old cure, accompanied by some other remedies, did its work. And then, " this morning the Queen paid me a visit in my bed-chamber. What do you think of that?" This information was not given to Lady Bradford only: " What do you think of receiving your Sovereign in slippers and dressing-gown?" he asked Lady Chesterfield in his correspondence with her.

How popular he was—or thought he was! " The Grand Duchess [the Duchess of Edinburgh who was a Russian Grand Duchess] is in despair at not seeing me. She has been reading Froude and wants to talk it over." But he remained invisible—except to his Faery. " You will understand from all this that I am a sort of prisoner of state, in the tower of a castle; royal servants come in and silently bring me my meals; a royal physician two or three times a day to feel my pulse, etc., and see whether I can possibly endure the tortures that await me. I am, in short, the man in the Iron Masque. . . ."

It must have been a great relief that in subsequent years he was spared the call to the Highlands. It was so much more comfortable to be in London and receiving bunches of blossoms from Osborne instead of surveying Lochnagar from a sick-room. To the Faery's floral tributes from Osborne he could reply in the flowers of speech that he never lacked. " Queen Titania, gathering flowers with her Court, in a soft and sea-girt isle, sending magic blossoms which they say turn the heads of those who receive them. . . ." Disraeli's head was only half-turned. He knew how to play his cards and where power lay. He inquired after the health and well-being of John Brown.

During the early eighteen-nineties, Campbell-Bannerman, as Minister of War in the Liberal Government, made three October appearances at Balmoral. To his wife he wrote of " the funniest life conceivable; like a convent. We meet at meals, breakfast at 9.45, lunch at 2.0, and dinner at 9.0, and, when we are finished, each of us is off to his cell (at least I to mine) and there is no common life except around a table." He had no grievance about the size of his room. (Harcourt, apparently, had called the Ministerial chamber a " hole.") C. B. described it as about the size of the turret-room at Belmont, but with a dressing-room added. The house in general he found " well warmed with hot water." He added, " I have a good fire and five new wax candles each night." With the aid of these he devoted his attention to the works of Emile Zola. *La Débacle* was one of them; it might fairly be called the required reading of a War Minister.

There was no agreement among guests about temperature. General Sir Henry Ponsonby, who became the Queen's Private Secretary in 1870, has described a keen dinner-time debate on the question as to how personal choice would go if one were permitted to vote for the North Pole or the Equator. Princess Beatrice had equatorial inclinations, but the Queen stood rigidly and frigidly by the Pole. " All doctors," she announced, " say that heat is unwholesome and cold wholesome." Lady Dalhousie, who called at Balmoral with Gladstone in 1884, and, despite the cold, " looked lovely " in the eyes of the General, replied to a question about the amenities of the Castle by the frank statement, " I never saw anything more uncomfortable or that I coveted less." Lady Mandeville, whom the General described as " blue with cold " was, in his opinion, " equally sour in her remarks about our Highland Palace."

Ponsonby was not a happy visitor, but perhaps not so unhappy as he has been made to seem; unfortunately his views and memories have come to us through the hands of his son, Arthur Ponsonby, who was far to the Left in politics and hardly a Balmoralist. If his father did make that remark about a Palace, he was being unfair. Balmoral was never meant to be a Palace. It had been planned as " our Highland home " and a centre of country-house parties; it was a base for Expeditions. Grandeur was not in mind. The General disliked field-sports and thought a day's shooting to be a dreadful waste of time. If he had to go out with the guns, he carried his reading matter with him. In his long and excellent service as Private Secretary he saw overmuch of Balmoral. The Queen stayed there too often and too long in his view and it was hard on him, as it was hard on all who did not fit easily into the world of Stag Parties, John Brown and the Ghillies' Ball, to have every year, and often twice a year, to make the necessary adjustment to the Deeside way of life.

Tastes differed greatly among the individual visitors. The Fresh Air School, the Gladstonian Hearties, with their zest for the Deer Forest or the less sanguinary pleasures of the Open Road, were naturally in favour of Balmoral. Many found it warm enough indoors. Campbell-Bannerman had been kept snug and Disraeli had found his room too snug for working in and had let the air in and the fire out. It is probably true that the Castle was at its least agreeable when the Queen's idea of procedure and of decorum had stiffened with the stiffening limbs of age and when she became testy and imperious.

The old spirit of " lacy ally," as Thackeray's Mr. Yellow-plush called it, the careless freedom of the Great Expeditions (incog.) and the informal nights of lodging in the mountain Shiels had gone. But even the General admitted that the Queen could be very gay and amusing on her good evenings. When Curtis's Band, whose members she was glad to discover were not foreigners but inhabitants of Kentish Town, played in the corridor and the strains of " Cavalliera," her favourite, were wafted in, she was touched to senti-mental raptures and she greatly enjoyed " the theatricals." Campbell-Bannerman ran into a spate of these in 1893 when a cluster of " stars " were assembled by command. The Bancrofts, Sir John Hare, Forbes-Robertson and Mary Rorke were called up from Aberdeen and they joined in a double programme with the ladies and gentlemen of the Household and other guests to present *A Scrap of Paper*, an old Anglicised French comedy done by the amateurs, and Sardou's *Diplomacy*, done by the professionals. Great fun, no doubt, but it did a little oppress the spirits of Campbell-Bannerman that he had to sit through both the Dress Rehearsal and the actual performance of these works. Considering the space and staging available and the necessity of putting on two productions in rapid succession, the Dress Rehearsal (at least of the amateurs) may well have proved to be rather elongated and chaotic.

Of all family gatherings seen at Balmoral the most remarkable was that of 1896. The congregation of Powers and of kin was indeed imposing. The now venerable Queen gathered to the Castle, which had been for thirty-five years the legacy of Albert's brain and enterprise and her house of dearest memories, no less than four generations of her blood. Of her own was a cousin, the Duke of Cambridge, of the second the Prince of Wales and other sons with their wives, of the third the Duke and Duchess of York and her grand-daughter Alix with her husband Nicholas II, Tsar of Russia, and of the fourth a boy of two, later to be Edward VIII. The Queen was glad to welcome Nicholas to the Braes of Mar: there was so much to discuss. She was immensely taken by young Master David, who tried to evict her from her chair, saying, "Get up, Gan-Gan." There was a fine new toy to play with, for Victoria had lived from the age of Landseer into that of "the pictures" and a film could be taken of the august party in motion on the terrace with the views of Lochnagar. There was the phonograph too. Progress, scientific and inventive, had come clicking and flickering and croaking to Balmoral.[1]

Diplomacy haunted the drives and the picnics and the planting of trees to keep the occasion green. Russia was so troublesome and could not the new young Tsar be per-suaded into better courses? His vexing, English-hating Foreign Minister, Prince Lobanoff, was dead and there was a chance to clear things up. Lord Salisbury was there. So surely something could be said and done about the Russian menace to India, something about the Russian attitude to the British occupation of Egypt, something about the Kaiser's goings-on, something about the Armenian mas-sacres. Lord Salisbury talked and talked. It was all most agreeable on the surface and most unsatisfactory below the surface, as so often happens when relations meet and national, as well as family, matters are discussed.

The Tsar was very gentle and very courteous and very

[1] *Queen Victoria* by E. F. Benson, p. 364.

vague. The Tsar was filmed and the Tsar prattled and the Tsar went on to Paris for more conversations and was horrified by the anti-clericalism then dominant in France. The Queen told Nicholas to tell the French that they really must not be hostile to the British. Again, a blank. He sent no answer. The great Balmoral gathering of 1896 was socially, no doubt, a great success; the clan had gathered, a portentous assemblage of the generations, but politically it achieved nothing at all. So the Queen had to console herself—and there was much that needed consolation, though the failure of eyesight had been checked—with the happy company of a great-grandchild, who was charming, and the reflection that she had reigned longer than any other sovereign of her country. And now she had to brace herself for the strains of the coming summer and the Festival of Empire, the Diamond Jubilee.

With the turn of the century and the new reign both Britain and Europe moved into an epoch of recurrent Crisis and Calamity. Von Moltke's remark about the oddness of this Highland seat as the home of far-reaching decisions at the highest level was amply justified. Never more so than when Mr. Sazonov, the Russian Foreign Minister, talked with Sir Edward Grey at Balmoral in the autumn of 1912. As Sazonov was touring the European capitals, King George V, having received a " Dearest Georgie " note from the Tsar which recommended the Minister as straightforward and honest, invited him to Balmoral together with Grey. The diplomats walked and talked about the Persian problem. They talked, too, about the menace of, and the defence against, German aggression. Grey was shy of committing the two Powers to Service Staff conversations, but he gave an assurance that Britain would not stand by and see France crushed by Germany. Grey's Radical critics were later to accuse him of evasions.

Sazonov was not, however, the plain-dealer that he was supposed to be. He might, for example, have taken the opportunity, during these Deeside sessions, to explain to Sir Edward that Russia had approved the secret pact between Serbia, Bulgaria and Greece which led to the Balkan War, the defeat of the Turks, and the infuriation of Austria. The Great War of 1914 was averted for two years by the subsequent appeasement of Austria at a London conference of Ambassadors. Nonetheless, it was more than a pity that Mr. Sazonov kept so much " under his hat " while he surveyed the Aberdeenshire scenery.

Next year was even more troubled. There was little peace of mind during the King's Scottish holiday of 1913. The Home Rule controversy was passing from contentious politics to threats of civil war and the King, with the sagacity of Lord Stamfordham at his side, had to devote much of his time and of his anxiety to correspondence from Balmoral with Mr. Asquith, not only on the immediate steps to be taken to prevent a recourse to violence but also on the constitutional relations between the Sovereign and the Prime Minister. Many of the Liberal Ministers and Conservative leaders were invited to the Castle, which became for a while a Westminster in little. Mr. Asquith himself was there for three days. He promised to begin private negotiations with Mr. Bonar Law, but was not hopeful of results. And so to another stormy summer of embittered altercations and threats and then, with overwhelming suddenness, to Sarajevo.

Balmoral can be seen in the nineteen-twenties and thirties as affording relief amid recurrent and severe anxieties. The visiting Minister was so often the representative of a Government in trouble, and August and September, instead of being months of calm, were frequently the Problem as well as the Shooting Season, with the horns of a dilemma rivalling the antlers in prominence of interest. One visualises the royal train at Ballater as frequently in readiness for a call to London. In 1919 there was a great, but abortive, Railway Strike. There was the Irish Agreement, so hardly won, in October, 1921. In the following year there was the Chanak Crisis when the nation, weary of war, suddenly found itself on the verge of war again. The steam was got up at Ballater, but Sir Charles Harington and Sir Horace Rumbold avoided a calamity. But if peace was saved Lloyd George was not, and he was never to hold office again. And so it went on. There was the economic and political crisis of 1931 and the King had to hurry back to London when the National Government was formed to bolster up the national economy. At that time he had his Prime Minister, when on vacation, reasonably adjacent to the premises. When George V retired to Balmoral, Mr. Ramsay Mac-Donald sought tranquillity rather farther north at Lossiemouth. George V, however, had never been as happy at Balmoral, much though he appreciated the moors, as he had been at Sandringham and he died amid the Norfolk levels and marshes to which his affections had so long been attached, at York Cottage and in the big house itself. A new generation was to occupy Balmoral.

Among the visitors to the Castle the tenants and ghillies have always been welcome on their special occasions. Queen Victoria never lost her zest for Highland dancing and participated even when age would seem to be warning her off that strenuous course. When that grave assemblage of guests, the members of the British Association, were invited to Balmoral in 1859, the reels and flings of the estate servants were an important contribution to the entertainment. The Ghillies' Ball became a great feature of the Castle life in Victorian times and so it has remained. This form of hospitality was early established and not at Balmoral only. How the Duchess of Kent loved to preside over such an occasion when she was at Abergeldie Castle has already been described. At Balmoral itself the Queen became so fond of this revel that it even became a matter for political disputation.

In 1871 there was much private comment and open criticism in the Press of the Queen's continued withdrawal from public life: her constant desire to be back in Scotland and her insistence on retirement to Deeside, even in times of political crisis or of visits by European monarchs and dignitaries, were attacked in the Press in a most candid and outspoken manner. The grumblers contrasted the dullness of Court life in England with the resort to gaiety in Scotland. The Queen was by no means well in 1871 and the eminent Lister had to be called from Edinburgh to Balmoral in order to operate on an abscess under the arm. So the resident and favourite physician, Sir William Jenner, could reasonably defend the royal seclusion on grounds of ill health. But it could still be inquired why, if she was unable to face a State Ball in London, she could so readily take part in the Ghillies' Ball in Aberdeenshire. Jenner replied that at the Ghillies' Ball she spoke to none, whereas in the ceremonial dances of the capital she would have to speak to many. This, it was urged, would be far more exhausting than taking the floor at Balmoral. Whether the Queen did or did not maintain such a rigid silence during the festivities of the

Crathie folk, she certainly never missed the affair if she could possibly attend it. If she, as Jenner stated, kept remarkably quiet, the general company did not, for the Ball was notably hilarious, at least in its later stages. The Queen took her share in the footwork and John Brown would be called on to be her partner once or twice in the gay evening.

She disliked anything to interfere with the entertainment of her Highlanders on her estate. The Ghillies' Ball was deemed an essential hospitality and an important part of the year's social routine. She resisted complaints about her reluctance to leave Scotland. The families of Private Secretaries were not welcomed in the Castle, which could be very irksome to the Secretaries themselves. The house of Abergeldie Mains was offered to Lady Ponsonby but not accepted or offered again. This establishment was later offered to two Assistant Private Secretaries, and occupied by them in alternate years. The pleasant house of Craigowan was built and occupied by the factor, Dr. Profeit, and later became the regular residence of the Private Secretary and his family.

Visitors were apt to find the Ghillies' Ball rough and noisy and preferred to escape from it if they could. But it was tactful to conform. General Ponsonby had to take his part and dance " a Hooligan " with the Queen. (The Hooligan was really the Hoolachan, defined as a noisy form of reel.) Other Englishmen, and possibly some Scots too, have found the screeching attending on the Hoolachan somewhat offensive to the ears and too easily overdone to be amusing or inspiriting. But apparently the Queen, if not vocal herself as Jenner alleged, was delighted by the vocalism of her visitors. She also gave and attended at Balmoral what were called the Quality Balls, for she had always liked to join a dance and would still tread a measure late in her life. But there seems to have been a particular fascination in what perhaps may be called the Quantity Balls with the revels of her local favourites in their native array and natively leaping. It must be remembered that Highlanders dance neatly as well as noisily. There would be grace as well as gallivanting in the Ghillies' Ball.

Mention of Jenner and of Lister reminds us that the visiting doctors had an important place in the Castle life. The Queen's addiction to more than a breath of cold air and her faith in the salutary affects of a shiver was not shared by all and there was usually some work for the medico to do, however buoyant the Queen's health might be. Sir William Jenner was for a long time influential and popular at Balmoral. He was not only a prudent counsellor, but gusty and voluble in conversation. He was allowed freedom of speech and of advice on other than clinical matters. Even those who did not care for his political explosions found him a welcome stimulant when the evening threatened to be dull.

In 1881 Dr. James Reid was appointed to be resident at Balmoral. He was an Aberdeenshire man and lived normally at Ellon on the East Coast of the County. He, like Jenner, managed to break down the harsh original rule that the Doctor was not a member of the Household and therefore should not dine with the Queen. His excellence in company earned him the promotion and his proficiency as a German scholar was an added recommendation. He became a great friend of the Private Secretary and his views were consulted on a number of topics. The medical man must have had plenty of strains and minor muscular troubles to attend to, for the mountain expeditions of guests on foot or on pony

led to slips and sprains. When Mrs. Gladstone, not asked
to Balmoral, was a guest with her husband in the neighbourhood she was taken for a long pony ride up Ben MacDhui
while her husband strode beside her. She complained later
that the long jolting made it painful to sit down in the
evening; such distresses only time could heal, but on the
whole the Doctor in the House has not been able to rely
on complete freedom from the first-aid box and the task
of prescribing.

So the story moves on through subsequent reigns, with
the kind of happiness which was originally sought and
found on Deeside still being reasonably shared between host
and guest. George V was a great host as well as an expert
on the moors and his Queen pursued her collecting of
beautiful craftsmanship and lovingly developed the gardens.
Edward VIII had, as a young man, preferred riding to
shooting: hence jogging on a pony to the butts or the
beginning of a stalk was not his favourite form of recreation.
He paid a dutiful visit to Deeside in the single year of his
unhappy reign and entertained, with Mrs. Simpson, the
dukes and duchesses of his choice and set. George VI and
his Queen were keen Balmoralists and their entertainment
was widely spread. Their welcome to the small acting
companies has been described. With his name, unfortunately, must be associated the saddest of all visitations to the
Castle, that of the doctors summoned in the autumn of
1951. With his name, too, must link the saddest of partings,
when the King drove out of the familiar gates to make his
last journey down Deeside, with the strong foreboding that
he would never come back.

Epilogue

NOT long ago one of the less responsible newspapers printed a foolish and malicious rumour that Balmoral had no future—at least as a royal residence. The Queen and the Duke of Edinburgh, it was alleged, had grown tired of it and would be glad to give it up. This was immediately denied. The fact is that Balmoral is now visited more than once a year, as it was in Queen Victoria's time. If other engagements permit, a short stay is made at the end of May or beginning of June. Such a visit serves as a welcome " breather " before the close-packed obligations of mid-summer in London and the Home Counties. At this time there are different recreations, good fishing instead of the autumnal shooting, and a glimpse of the country-side in quite another hue from that of its empurpled September. The vivid greens of the late Scottish spring are particularly beautiful in a region of many birches and larches. Abandon this? It is not usual to increase the habitation of a place one is eager to leave. Moreover, there are other considerations than those of personal pleasure. It would be a blow to Scottish feelings—and the Scots are sensitive on such matters—if it were decided that the holidays, so long enjoyed in Aberdeenshire, were to be spent elsewhere. The holidays, incidentally, often include some dutiful service in the cities of Scottish occasions where industrial enterprise is on exhibition and royal patronage is much valued.

So it continues. The Queen, in residence at Balmoral, is a busy woman. To talk of holidays may be misleading. She has her dispatches to read day by day. The Private Secretary, recently Sir Alan Lascelles, now Sir Michael Adeane, is kept occupied with the heavy official correspondence—the Castle needs a Post Office of its own—and with all the arrangements upon which a quick decision is needed. Modern communications make light of the six hundred miles once so complained of by Ministers, but the ease of communications adds to the number of them. So there is plenty to be done; but the Queen always finds time to spend some hours with her children and usually she drives out with the other ladies at midday to a picnic lunch on the moors where the men are shooting. Queen Elizabeth proved herself an excellent shot with a rifle and a keen stalker before her marriage and had many good " heads " to her credit. Since the birth of her children she has diminished her sporting activities. Members of the family are regularly at Birkhall and there are house-parties arriving in succession at Balmoral.

It is a pity that the climate, which was the first attraction to Queen Victoria, has tended in recent years to be on less good behaviour. But so have our summers in general. The long spells of dry, sunny weather, the news of which made a powerful magnet when they came to Queen Victoria during her stay in the rain-swept west, have not been constantly in attendance. Scottish Septembers have been losing the radiant reputation which once they held and the Braemar Gathering has been especially unlucky. On the day of the Games in 1954 the massing of the low and leaden clouds in a drenched

Deeside was the more unkind since there was a brilliant afternoon in North Aberdeenshire, as I discovered by making a visit to the Deveron instead of staying by the Dee.

One recent Scottish calamity Balmoral shared to the full. That was the colossal hurricane of January, 1953. While the *Princess Victoria* was stricken by the tempest and sank in the Irish Sea, and while the East Coast of England and the shores of Holland were suffering their terrible ordeal by sea-water owing to the combination of high tides and a raging gale from the north, Scotland was assaulted in an unprecedented way. It was fortunate in losing no lives through the ferocious tornado which ravaged the north and east of the country in particular. But the destruction of valuable timber was on a gigantic scale. In two hours Scotland lost trees by the million; five million were felled in the region between Inverness and Aberdeen alone. It was the greatest forestry disaster in the recorded history of the country. The conifers, with their shallow roots, were the most numerous casualties. It was the finest that were the worst smitten. The taller the tree the greater the exposure and the risk. So, fortunately, many of the younger woods escaped severe damage, which was lucky for the Forestry Commission with its large number of recent plantations.

On the Balmoral estate, even in comparatively sheltered spots, great swathes were cut in the woodlands. The hurricane worked in a most freakish way, swirling round hillsides and leaving belts of utter desolation. In one area to the south of the Castle I saw whole acres of timber which had been mown down with not a tree left standing. All along Deeside, from the Cairngorms to Aberdeen, there remained, on one estate after another, a vast tangle of prostrate trunks and a jungle of broken branches and uptorn roots. Such a jungle was a natural swarming-ground for all sorts of pests, from the beetles and weevils in the decaying wood to the rabbits for whom such excellent cover was provided among the débris. The loss of property and the labours of clearance and disposal were huge and resolutely faced. It was heartbreaking to see the natural wealth of the country thus dissipated and Balmoral suffered along with all the Deeside forests and woodlands; I noted much shocking damage all along the main road and Glentanar was another area to be cruelly stripped. The Castle of Balmoral, though by no means exposed, lost some of its protective timber, a benefit, in its way, to sightseers, but not to those residents who naturally seek in their Highland vacation an escape from the peeping crowds to which they are continually exposed elsewhere.

Among Balmoral's more recent amenities is a fascinating little golf-course over up-and-down parkland and with holes of cunning invention. So those guests who are indisposed for the fatigues of the stalk can take their exercise in a gentler and less lethal manner. The provision of the Castle's pleasures continues to be ample and, during the summer while the house is not being used, there is a day a week in which the public can enjoy a walk in the grounds for a small entry fee which goes to charity.

A backward glance over the Castle's century of its new life confirms the foolishness of the charges that are still occasionally levelled by the more peevish type of Scottish writer when he inveighs against the so-called " Balmorality." For example, the suggestion, cited in my first chapter, that the royal settlement in Deeside could be associated with the

decline of Highland life and even with the nefarious clearances of the crofters to create unpopulated sheep-ranches
and deer forests, is seen to be utterly absurd. The whole of
the Highland territories have suffered a severe decline of
population during the last fifty years and the process has
unhappily continued during the twenty years between the
Census of 1931 and that of 1951. The Islands have lost
most grievously: even in those two decades the island of
Coll, for example, lost a third of its inhabitants, whose total
fell from 300 to 200. It is astonishing now to read of the
great numbers who managed to exist even in the most barren
regions two hundred years ago; but it was an existence with
a very low standard of housing, and lacking even the most
elementary comforts. The swarms of hovel-dwelling
Tinchels available three and a half centuries ago for the
great huntings in the Braes of Mar seem strange to the
modern reader who knows the comparatively empty
glens. But a Tinchel's way of living would not be popular
now.

It was the lure of town-life with its money and its pleasures,
often garish and even vulgar but none the less actual and
beckoning, that took many from the land. Where there were
Clearances it was usually the Highland landlord who was
thus brutal to his own people and not the alien lord. The
famous Canadian Boat Song (from the Gaelic, the translator's
name still disputed)[1] which appeared in the *Noctes Am-
brosianae* in the September issue of Blackwood's Magazine
in 1829 (well before the royal occupation of Balmoral)
does not accuse the English aristocracy of the new desolation.

[1] The translation has been ascribed with some plausibility to the joint hands
of Sir Walter Scott and J. G. Lockhart.

When the bold kindred, in the time long-vanished,
Conquered the soil and fortified the keep,
No seer foretold the children would be banished
That a degenerate Lord might boast his sheep.

The Lord was the old owner, not the new arrival.

The joint parish of Crathie and Braemar, an enormous area of more than 180,000 acres, mostly barren mountain, reaching away to the borders of Banffshire, Inverness-shire and Perthshire, and including three summits of over 4,000 feet, appears to have reached its maximum population of 2,671 in 1755, when Dr. Webster made a return to the Government. In 1831 this had fallen to 1,808 and since then the diminution has gone on, but not at anything like the rate obtaining in other similar regions. Another 500 had gone between 1831 and 1931, but now the numbers are actually going up. The Census of 1951 recorded a slight rise in this parish, while the " crofters' county " of Sutherland showed a loss of 2,500 from the 1931 total of 15,300 in its " land-ward " areas. The decrease in the Islands was even more severe: many which had seven or eight hundred inhabitants in the eighteenth century are now down to three hundred or two or less. So the Balmoral area has certainly not been " cleared " to add to the pleasures of the few and the Castle estates have been greatly improved both in the matter of housing and of use of the small amount of land where farming is possible.

The desire to follow royalty inevitably increased the value of other Deeside properties and brought in wealthy owners (or tenants) from the South. But that they have been as oppressive as the " degenerate Lords " arraigned in the old song or indeed oppressive at all cannot be maintained.

Deeside has acquired a seigneurial look, but it has had a general prosperity as well and it is against all reason to suppose that Queen Victoria, who idealised the local population to the point of sentimentality, would have in any way encouraged their ill-treatment or dispersal. The introduction of English industrial wealth was in some cases an advantage, leading to better accommodation of the poorer tenants and good upkeep of the estates. No doubt it is galling to a Scottish Nationalist of the extreme type or to the political theorist of the Left, who assumes that wealth and wickedness always go together, to see a most beautiful part of the country much beset by the invading sportsman or tourist. But the whole situation must be regarded with a fair sense of proportion. Those deer-fences may offend his eye, but they are protection for the farmer and in the deer-forest of Balmoral itself there are the rights of way for all to take, if they wish to climb Lochnagar or strike southward into Angus.

The occupation of Balmoral II and the building of Balmoral III occurred at a time when Scottish life did need stimulation and Scottish confidence did require to be renewed. Royal attention to the Northern Kingdom was not primarily a piece of policy; but, if only as a by-product, it served to remind the English that something does happen north of the Tweed, a fact which, to judge by the amount of Scottish news printed in English newspapers, is generally overlooked. The eighteen-forties and eighteen-fifties were, for Scotland, a period of rapid industrial advancement in the urban centre of the land where were the minerals to be exploited and the harbours to further trade. But the great burst of intellectual vitality which had given Edinburgh a fair claim to its title of Modern Athens had died down. The

Edinburgh Review had ceased to be its old self. The two greatest contributors to the *Review*, Macaulay and Brougham, both partially Scottish, had gone to London. The scattering of the Scots from a country whose old capital had long ceased to be the centre of a self-governing nation and had lost some at least of its repute as the forum of the philosophers, the scholars and the wits, was proceeding widely and rapidly. There was progressive Anglicisation of Scottish talent.

As part of his survey of Scotland during the nineteenth century in his book on *Scottish and Welsh Nationalism*, Sir Reginald Coupland has shown in how many cases the born Scot became in Victorian times the successful Englishman or European. Gladstone was hardly ever thought of as Scottish: nor was Ruskin, who seemingly preferred the romantic scenery of the English Lakes to that of Tayside where his boyhood had been so happy, and happy in contrast to the rest of his uneasy life. Carlyle went south to think Teutonically and to be the sage of Chelsea. Coupland mentions not only Gladstone as one of the " Lost Scots," but John Stuart Mill. His father was purely Scottish, an Angus man, but young Mill never mentioned Scotland again in his Autobiography after allusion to that fact of his paternity. Macaulay's father occupied the Manse at Inveraray, but, despite his name and his origin, the son talked of his home-sickness for England when in India and often did not use the term Britain when writing of the United Kingdoms; he lumped Scotland in as a bit of " England." This seems less than tactful now; but it was a common habit then.

There was a decline, too, in the Scottish arts. The Scottish novel, carried to the heights by Sir Walter Scott and maintained at a considerable altitude by John Galt, was no longer being written at any such level. There is a curious and melancholy gap between the end of Scott and Galt and the beginning of Stevenson. If the Kailyarders must be derided, at least it can be said on their behalf that they did not leave Scotland forgotten or unrecorded. The great age of Scottish painting and portraiture had also passed with Raeburn and Wilkie, and native poetry could no longer provide the energy and gusto of Burns, Hogg and Tannahill. The population of the lonely regions ebbed and the increase of numbers in the towns was partly met with an eager escape to find new careers either in the south or overseas. This was certainly true of the young, bursary-winning scholars of the time; many of them had had so hard a childhood and so austere an academic life that they had some reason for seeking sweetness and light in the richer lands and looking back on Scotland as the hard nurse or parent whose poverty and severity left bleak memories.

These sons of the manse and the farm were everywhere getting on and getting out. Queen Victoria chose to find in Scotland her favourite home and her dear Paradise just when so many Scots were regarding it as a good place to leave. It is a little hard that she should be blamed by the critics of Balmorality for paying their country the compliment of loving it when the young natives of talent and of ambition were so eagerly leaving it. She came and she stayed. She, at any rate, was not eager to forget the very title of Scotland and to annex it in her vocabulary as an English province. The *Journals* continually stress the essential differences between Scotland and England and between the Scots and the English. She did not disparage the latter by her deep affection for the former. As Coupland has well put it:[1]

" She forged a personal link between the British monarchy and Scotland such as none of her predecessors since the Union had even thought of. She created her second son Duke of Edinburgh in 1866—the first royal dukedom with a Scottish title. When her fourth and youngest son was born in 1853, she gave him " Duncan " for his second Christian name as " a compliment to dear Scotland," and created him Duke of Albany in 1881; and the second Duke received at his grandmother's bidding the names " Charles Edward " in memory of the Young Pretender. These delicacies of nomenclature were not mere trifles."

She spent far more of her time in Scotland than some of her Ministers and Private Secretaries thought politic or agreeable. Time and again the return to " our dear Scotland " was made despite the pressure of London counsel to the contrary. It cannot, of course, be argued that the Queen's obstinate maintenance of her long Balmoral visits had a direct influence in countering the decline of Scottish vitality and self-reliance during the middle of the nineteenth century. But her resolution to spend so much of her time in Scotland was an assertion, most valuable at that period, of Scotland's qualities and fascinations.

That in her devotion to the Highlands there were errors of taste, or errors of taste by the standards of to-day, can fairly be argued. She did not merely like her Deeside home and its surroundings; she loved them, and love is an immoderate passion. Hence the infection by Tartanitis, the

---

[1] *Scottish and Welsh Nationalism*, p. 272.

invention of a new tartan, and the inordinate use of old ones. One period will always smile at in a superior way or decry with a contemptuous sneer the taste of that closely preceding it. The middle of the nineteenth century was the epoch of the Picturesque Traveller; the adjective was transferred in guide-books from the scene itself to the person viewing it. One feature of the Picturesque Age was the selection of certain aspects of country or of people which seemed unusual and " old world "; ruins were deemed more beautiful than buildings unimpaired; barren solitudes were preferable to cultivated land. The Picturesque painters have, because of their mixture of realism with romance, been dismissed by the modern devotees of distortion and abstraction as mere practitioners of coloured photography. But photography is much more objective than painting. The landscape artists of the Ben-and-Glen School, so much favoured in the middle and late-Victorian years, were extremely selective; they picked out those elements of the scene which were deemed to be Picturesque; hence there was the constant repetition of the Highland cattle paddling in the loch beneath the misty peak, of the triumphs of the sportsmen, or of the sheep in the snow. We find these things tiresome and prefer to see landscape without this repeated emphasis on a few fashionable items. We have ceased to be Picturesque Travellers and many now prefer to see the country-side analysed into geometrical forms or made symbolic of tumultuous natural forces. Such cool dissection naturally has no sympathy with the raptures of our grandfathers over the lochs, peaks, and animal life, which were fondly depicted in the age of Landseer's immense popularity. No sovereign has been more violently dethroned than the Monarch of the Glen.

The third Balmoral was built by and for the generation of Picturesque Travellers with their relish for the curious, the antique, the brightly colourful. It was true to the dominant spirit of its age and, if the Picturesque was to be favoured, the Castle could hardly have been better sited or more enthusiastically decorated. That fashion will retrace its steps and that a new form of the Picturesque will before long be admitted to respect and to enjoyment is most probable. However that may be, it is ridiculous to overlook the happiness which the third Balmoral conferred on its creators and on most of their descendants, merely because there was, to begin with, an excess of tartan in the upholstery and the wallpapers, because the pictorial art of the time was founded on the Royal Academicians' belief that " every picture tells a story," and because of their belief that the story should be intelligibly conveyed in line and colour with due regard to the romantic appreciation of those forms and hues indiscoverable in the ordinary urban scene.

One further point may be urged on behalf of the early devotees of the Paradise. The first Picturesque Travellers in Switzerland or the Lake District were not adventurous; they proceeded by coach, guide-book in hand, visiting the starred beauty spots, admiring the wonders of Nature, and agreeing that the old adjective " horrid," which the eighteenth century had so constantly applied to the mountains, must now be radically altered. The horrid had become the superb, the sublime, or the stupendous. Awe was no longer fright, the fright which had assailed Defoe even at the spectacle of a rapidly-flowing river. It was a reverent wonder. But the wonder stopped at the glory of the spectacle: it did not call for further and strenuous investigation. Those who were entranced by the Lakes stayed securely on the shore; those who were entranced by the peaks did not assault them. The rocks had ceased to be horrid; but that did not make them friendly or familiar. They were a delectable skyline. They were journey's end.

The practice of admiration set at Balmoral was not so timid or so sluggish. The new occupants were not content to leave the Picturesque unprobed. Queen Victoria was, as we have seen, an active investigator. She shared the idea of all explorers that a mountain is there to be mastered and up she would go so long as her age and strength were capable. The Great Expeditions were the summit of her felicity, and many of those who have been guests at Balmoral ever since have had to realise that the sports of the Highlands are not to be followed without physical fitness and endurance. The royal children playing on the lawns and in the woods of the Castle to-day are unlikely to be Picturesque Travellers when they are old enough to go farther afield in search of that very active and even exacting happiness which was being sought and captured by their forebears a hundred years ago. It would have added largely to the pleasure of Queen Victoria if she had known that, at the centenary of her entrance to her own and her husband's creation, the very young heir to her throne and also to her " Highland home " would be called Prince Charles.

Some Books Consulted

Leaves from the Journal of Our Life in the Highlands, Smith Elder, now John Murray

More Leaves from the Journal of A Life in the Highlands, Smith Elder, now John Murray

Queen Victoria by Lytton Strachey, Chatto & Windus.

Queen Victoria by E. F. Benson, Longmans

Victoria of England by Dr. Edith Sitwell, Faber

Queen Victoria's Letters edited by Sir Sidney Lee, John Murray

The Life of the Prince Consort by Sir Theodore Martin, Smith Elder

The Prince Consort by Roger Fulford, Macmillan

Henry Ponsonby by Sir Arthur Ponsonby, Macmillan

Sidelights on Queen Victoria by Sir Frederick Ponsonby, Macmillan

Recollections of Three Reigns by Sir Frederick Ponsonby, Eyre & Spottiswoode

Queen Victoria and John Brown by E. E. P. Tisdall, Stanley Paul

Edward VII by Sir Sidney Lee, Macmillan

George V by Harold Nicolson, Constable

George V by John Gore, Constable

The Life of Gladstone by John Morley, Macmillan

The Life of Benjamin Disraeli by Monypenny & Buckle, John Murray

The Pennyles Pilgrimage by John Taylor, E. Allde, 1618

A Tour of Scotland by Thomas Pennant, printed for B. White

The Drove Roads of Scotland by A. R. B. Haldane, Nelson

A Year of Space by Eric Linklater, Macmillan

Crathie and Braemar by Rev. John Stirton, Milne & Hutchinson, Aberdeen

SOME BOOKS CONSULTED

Recollections of a Royal Parish by Patricia Lindsay, John Murray

Balmoral Castle and Crathie Kirk by W. Douglas Simpson, Mearns Publications, Aberdeen

Welsh and Scottish Nationalism by Sir Reginald Coupland, Collins

Life Among the Scots by Janet Adam Smith, Collins

The Sporting Rifle by " The Ruffle," Betchworth

Deer-Stalking in the Forest of Atholl by William Scope (1841), John Murray

The Scottish Annual, and Book of the Braemar Gathering (Several Years) by many Contributors, printed by Herald Press, Arbroath

Travelling Players by Eleanor Elder, Muller

Victoria Regina by Laurence Housman, Cape

The Golden Sovereign by Laurence Housman, Cape

Shakespeare Rediscovered by Clara Longworth de Chambrun, Scribners

Who's Who in the Theatre 1952, edited by the late John Parker, Pitman

Scotland in Quest of Her Youth, A Scrutiny, edited by David Cleghorn Thomson, Oliver & Boyd

My Scotland by A. G. Macdonell, Jarrold

Barrie and the Kailyard School by George Blake, Arthur Barker

INDEX